EXPERIENCERS
Conscious Contactees

Edited By

Janet Kira Lessin

Featuring

Russell Scott Brinegar, Joan Hangarter, Miesha Johnston, Barbara Jean Lindsey, Melinda Leslie, Hildegard Gmeiner, Sasha Alex Lessin, Ph.D., Karen Christine Patrick, Korey Lavoie, Reverend John M. Polk, Bret Colin Sheppard, Sherry Wilde, Rebecca Hardcastle Wright

EXPERIENCERS CONSCIOUS CONTACTEES

Copyright © 2017 Janet Kira Lessin

All rights reserved.

ISBN-10: 1541220757
ISBN-13: 978-1541220751

DEDICATION

To my beloved husband, Sasha Alex Lessin, Ph. D. and my magical Maui cats without whom there are barely a reason to get out of bed. To my family, my brother Bill and Sister Louise who have been with me since the beginning of this long, wild ride. To all my dear ones in the Aquarian Radio Network who are hobbits, dwarves, elves and wizards that trek with me through Middle Earth, fight demons and dragons as we make our way to Mordor where together, we set our people free. We are legion.

EXPERIENCERS CONSCIOUS CONTACTEES

CONTENTS

Acknowledgments   *i*
Forward   *iii*

1. *I Like Ike*   7
   Janet Kira Lessin

2. *Benefit From Extraterrestrial Contact*   22
   Sasha Lessin, Ph. D.

3. *Truth Be Told: I Am An Experiencer*   49
   Karen Christine Patrick

4. *Once And Future Art*   71
   Bret Colin Sheppard

5. *The Blue Beings*   88
   Rev. John Polk

6. *Time To Be Human*   104
   Janet Kira Lessin

7. *Alien Encounters*   110
   Korey Lavoie

8. *Beyond The Space Time Continuum: Where Am I?*   130
   Rebecca Hardcastle Wright

9. *The Story Of Joan Of Angels*   150
   Joan Hangarter

10	*Near Death* Russell Brinegar	161
11	*Experiences Of A Walk-In From Bootes Andromeda Galaxy* Hildegard Gmeiner	175
12	*Covert Abduction : Autobiography Of Mind Control* Miesha Johnston	204
13	*Detour: The Abduction Experience Of Melinda Leslie And Two Friends* Melinda Leslie	243
14	*The South Point UFO Experience* Barbara Jean Lindsey	257
15	*The Story Behind the Forgotten Promise* Sherry Wilde	271
16	*Levitating Baby* Janet Kira Lessin	279
17	The Grim Reaper Janet Kira Lessin	291
18	*Edgar Mitchell Foundation for Research Into Extraterrestrial Encounters*	308
18	*Epilogue*	311
19	*About the Editor*	314

EXPERIENCERS CONSCIOUS CONTACTEES

ACKNOWLEDGMENTS

Special thanks to Russell Scott Brinegar, Joan Hangarter, Miesha Johnston, Barbara Jean Lindsey, Melinda Leslie, Hildegard Gmeiner, Sasha Alex Lessin, Ph.D. Karen Christine Patrick, Korey Lavoie, Reverend John M. Polk, Bret Colin Sheppard, Sherry Wilde, Rebecca Hardcastle Wright who contributed to Volume I of the experiencers anthology series.

Also I'd like to extend a special thank you to those who already sent me your chapters and for those who will contribute to this ongoing series. Your stories wake up humanity. We are disclosure. We couldn't do it without you.

Our only and best hope is that those who are brave enough to come out of the closet and tell their tales realize the importance of their transparency and honesty. Your testimonials work. You're opening eyes, waking people up. Keep up the good work.

Thanks to all who came on our many shows on the Aquarian Radio network over the years. Drop us a line. We'd love to have you back.

Many thanks also to those who've invited us on their radio and television shows. We're honored. We appreciate all those who put on conferences and invite us to speak or allow us to purchase a vendor table and talk to all of you who seek us out. We recognize your hard work. You're awesome.

Thanks also to those who attend and come to listen. Without you there would be no ears to hear, no eyes to see. We need you for together we learn from each other.

We ask that you contribute so that we might all discover the truth (or at least a close facsimile that will work for the majority of humankind on that long road in search of the win-for-all). For some the road to personal disclosure is paved with hardship and repercussions. We honor you, support you as you overcome and do the right thing.

Without you we'd be lost. You know who you are. We may not have met (yet) in person in this lifetime. But we are eternally connected on the soul level.

All of you represent the many pieces in the universal puzzle and we need every single one of you or the puzzle remains incomplete. Without you there would be no disclosure and we need disclosure to survive as a species and save mother Earth.

FORWARD
Sasha Alex Lessin, Ph.D.

Let yourself identify with each writer in this book. With each, experience extraterrestrial encounters, psychic intuitions, timetravel. As you read, empathize with the writer so totally that you feel like you have the writer's experience yourself. Then notice if the writer's experience resonates with what you in your own life felt, saw, heard or intuited. Interlife, pastlife, futurelife and simultaneous-life experiences the writers share stir up scenes you now recall or remember more than before.

Janet Kira Lessin and her writers invite you to join their community of ambassadors of more loving consciousness. Tune into the benign awarenesses in space, other dimensions, Inner Earth and your very own DNA. Open to beings that urge us to survive, stop suffering, thrive and ascend to a loving, spiritually-oriented cooperative planet.

Experiencers until the recent past kept their encounters private to avoid ridicule, punishment or even pluralistic ignorance of how many millions have had ET, paranormal or spiritual experiences. They, and you too maybe have had 3D encounters, near death experiences, rebirths, remote views, astral visits, guide visitations, ghosts communication, teleportation, entheogenic journeys, hypnotic regressions and deep meditations. You've boarded alien craft, been on Admiralty, Corporate and extraterrestrial bases.

Together, let us lower the veils of the perverted paradigm that shroud the loving oneness that is our spirit-right. Remember who we really are beneath the matrix; our souls remember we are one with each other and all.

EXPERIENCERS CONSCIOUS CONTACTEES

EXPERIENCERS CONSCIOUS CONTACTEES

I LIKE IKE
Janet Kira Lessin

I arrived on Earth born into human form in February 1954, the month Eisenhower was president, the month Ike met with aliens. I don't believe my arrival on Earth at that historical time was coincidence since my soul origination is not from this planet and my body is a human/alien hybrid.

Under the pretext that he had to undergo emergency dental surgery, President Dwight Eisenhower was secretly whisked away to Edwards Air Force Base and not seen publically again until the following Sunday when appeared at a church service in Los Angeles. At Edwards Ike held a secret meeting with extraterrestrial visitors during the early hours of February 21, 1954, while officially he was on vacation to Palm Springs, California.

The President's sudden and mysterious disappearance was so unusual the media speculated Ike was ill or had died and the rumors became so intense the president's press secretary, James Haggerty, told reporters at a press conference that Ike damaged a tooth cap while eating fried chicken and had to undergo emergency surgery.

In UFO conspiracy lore, Eisenhower thus became the first American president to have direct contact with extraterrestrials. But for those who do their homework, stories abound that other presidents, from Washington who say angels to Truman's encounters with the Roswell aliens, trump Eisenhower's claim to fame as the first to meet with aliens.

However, the meeting that took place at Edwards Air Force Base in southern California during the early hours of February 21 in 1954 was significant in that it was the first in a series of meetings that culminated with the signing of a treaty between the U.S. government and an extraterrestrial race called the Greys.

In the First Contact secret meeting Ike met with the Nordic aliens who are called "the Nordics" due to their fair hair, blue eyes and white skin. They are a faction of the Pleiadians, an advanced extraterrestrial race from the Pleiades star. They may also be the Anunnaki who originate from Nibiru. They could also be the Tall Whites, who are human/Anunnaki hybrids.

EXPERIENCERS CONSCIOUS CONTACTEES

Eyewitness Gerald Light, a writer and leading member of the community dedicated to metaphysical research wrote a letter dated April 16, 1954, to Meade Layne, Director of Borderland Sciences Research Foundation. Light, one of a group of community leaders present at the First Contact meeting, witnessed extraterrestrials at Edwards Air Force Base.

Light wrote to Layne that he recently returned from Muroc Airfield (now Edward Air Force Base) and called the aliens Etherians. Light said the aliens are giving permission and assistance to the Air Force to study at least five separate and distinct types of aircraft. These alien UFOs are stored at the facility for reverse-engineering studies.

The officials present at the meeting were uncertain how to respond to the aliens. Paranoid due to the Cold War, they feared the aliens would approach the Soviets if the Americans spurned them.

Perhaps those fears led Eisenhower to reject the proposals of the Nordic aliens and sign a treaty with the Greys, who made an exclusive offer to transfer their technology only to the United States.

In 1953 astronomers discovered a fleet of huge UFOs approaching Earth which were initially mistaken for asteroids. Whistle-blower William Cooper, a former naval intelligence officer said signals were intercepted under Project Sigma just before the UFOs went into high orbit. Project Plato was launched to receive the aliens and hold talks.

But before the original group of aliens in a huge UFO fleet could land, a different alien race contacted the U.S government and warned against the first group of aliens. Talks with the first group failed after they demanded nuclear disarmament. They warned that humanity was on a path to self-destruction and proposed to help humans develop a peaceful path to spiritual fulfillment.

The Eisenhower administration rejected the overtures from the Nordic aliens and signed a treaty at Holloman Air Force Base in New Mexico later in 1954 with the Greys because the U.S. government was primarily interested in gaining access to advanced alien technology.

Other whistle-blowers confirmed the First Contact meetings. Former retired U.S. Marine Corps Sergeant Charles Suggs claimed his father, a senior naval officer, attended the First Contact meeting with the Nordic aliens in February 1954. Former air pilot John Lear, the son of the builder of the Lear Jet, William Lear, confirmed that two alien races had been involved in the First Contact meetings.

Robert Dean, a former intelligence officer, says Nordic aliens are humanoid. One species of Greys appears as tall humanoids with pale white skin, large eyes, large head, and spindly limbs and can stand up to nine feet tall. Some come from the constellation of Orion and others come from a planet in the star system Zeta Reticuli.

EXPERIENCERS CONSCIOUS CONTACTEES

Under extreme conditions of secrecy, the Greys agreed to non-interference in human affairs in exchange for accommodation on Earth and in return, they'd furnish the U.S. government with advanced technology which would help the U.S. stay ahead of enemy nations. They also agreed they'd not approach nor create treaties with any other nations.

Underground bases either existed previously and/or additional bases were constructed. Phil Schneider worked as a geological engineer employed by a private company contracted to build underground bases in Dulce. He revealed that the treaty agreement allowed the Greys to abduct a limited number of humans for medical research and experiments. But the Greys lied and violated the abduction agreement, as evident by the extreme number of abductions reported by experiencers worldwide.

I am one of those experiencers. While I've experienced contact that may be interpreted as abductions, I remember consciously that I chose to send my soul into this avatar at this time to be a part of this grand experiment in consciousness.

I belong to a subcategory of experiencers who have conscious recall. While I don't have to undergo hypnosis to remember what happened to me, I do work with my hypnotherapist to recall details I may have suppressed and to work through my emotions, negative, positive and everything in between to gain clarity and greater understanding of what it means personally and as a researcher to understand the experiencer phenomenon in general.

I am a multidimensional being having many simultaneous incarnations and exist on many levels, realms, dimensions and planets. I came here February 1954, sent a thread of my consciousness into the fetus and body of the baby known as Janet so that I might better understand what human life is like. The body I inhabit is a hybrid which is not only part Anunnaki and human, but is also from the House of Enki and is directly descended from Enki and Ninmah.

In addition, I was also part of that envoy that presented itself to Ike. I am a very old Anunnaki soul who's dedicated to the preservation of human life and the many lifeforms and features on this incredibly beautiful planet. Earth is my project, a planet I've personally terraformed in my existences as both Joy, a being that resides 39 degrees on the right side of God and as Ki'Ra, a Galzu who came down through the dimensions to 3D physicality in an avatar to oversee the project with my team millions of years ago.

We perhaps could have used a different approach with Ike rather than demand he cease using nuclear weapons. Humans are like children who play with matches and are about to set the house on fire. But this story is incomplete and does not include what later unfolded to set the record straight. We do have our treaties in place and interact with humans on many levels on a daily basis. I'm getting ahead of myself.

Janet's here as an ambassador to awaken not only herself, as she agreed to partial amnesia in order to cope and be more effective. How better to deal with humans than become one?

Bottom line, we walk among you. Some of us are fully awake and aware. Some are not even beginning to awaken. But most are aware on some level and the smarter, more cautious ones hold their tongues till others, like perhaps you the reader are ready to listen and emphasize with their plight. Humans are complex beings, believe some things they should not and don't believe things they should.

So please have patience with us as we gather our wits about us to figure the best way to light your fires and awaken you to the true history of your existence without totally blowing your minds.

While I lack some of the details of why my soul chose to join with this avatar at this time, I do know that a part of me, my "Oversoul" if you will, knows all and knows now is the time, the time is now and all's perfect and is proceeding in divine perfection.

Validation of my personal truth always finds me. About 45 years after my birth a whistleblower contacted me on the internet and said he had been watching me all my life. He claimed there was a whole unit dedicated to studying me in a secret section of a naval base in Virginia. He Said, "We tracked you as you were coming in from the spiritual realm to your body to be born here on this earth."

Years later that scene was enacted in a movie produced by director Stephen Spielberg called "Taken". I was guided by spirit to rent the series and binge watch all 20 hours in less than a week.

Years later I met another experiencer whose story also resembles many elements included in the "Taken" series. In following chapters we'll reveal how our lives are entwined in ways that to this day continue to reveal themselves and shock us.

We also reveal in the chapters ahead how we were led to our soul mates which not only gave us love, romance and companionship, but also provided additional key elements to our awakening and revelations about who we really are and our roles in the ascension process for humanity and this world.

I remember many of my past and concurrent lives and levels of existence. I'm shown through downloads and interactions with extraterrestrials the true dynamics of human interactions with non-Earth based life forms. We in conjunction with Source co-created this continuum and all life and things within it for our growth, development and entertainment. We diversify and co-create with one another and God Source. We are everything and all.

In this book I own all aspects of myself and present

myself and the true complexity of my being to you so you might better understand and internalize that we are all of the above. I am aware of my existence as Joy, Ki'Ra, Ninmah, Janet and many other beings incarnate and not that were born, lived and died and some who've never sub parsed from the totality of existence into human form.

I am just like you and you are just the same as I am a multi-dimensional being with numerous lifetimes and levels of existence. The only difference between you and I is that I have become aware of my many lives and you may remain in the program that limits your awareness of your many selves. I invite you to awaken to your full potential.

To model it, I shall begin with myself to show you and the world how we awaken everyone, reconnect with Source, know our oneness (not simply believe) and create a world which honors all life and this planet because we now remember and now feel and emphasize with everyone and everything.

I came down to this planet in February 1954 in two ways. First on February 6th at 9:20 PM Eastern time in Pittsburgh, PA I was born into a human baby form so like others who came before and chose human avatars in order to better understand what it's like to live a lifetime as a human.

Secondly members of my family, crew and staff

volunteered to meet with Eisenhower that same month and while he rejected us (as we expected) we came back, have always been here and never left.

Regardless of how our children perceive us or even treat us, we remain devoted to your evolution as you literally are us and we you, and will continue to guide and love you. We are most loyal. While some members of my species act less than kind and treat humans like slaves, we realize these dynamics exist to motivate humanity to create technologies and grow.

Ultimately we are parents who supervise our children as they play with matches. In this case the children are human and the matches are nuclear. Your nukes could end all life on this planet.

I have personally made mistakes around nuclear weapons. When the council met to stop Marduk, I voted for the bombing of Sodom and Gomorrah. At that time I believed there were no other options to save both our worlds. Marduk had run amok, threatened to end all we knew and so believing that was the only option, I voted to end it all in the worst possible way.

My brother and husband, Enki, was the only one who held fast and walked out rather than vote. In the end my sister, Bau who was also married to my eldest son, Ninurta perished in the holocaust. My losses were painful and personal. I am dedicated and will not permit such destruction again.

After nukes were used by humans, we became aware how brilliant our children are and now carefully pay attention. We do interfere and while there are parts we allow based on universal spiritual laws of non-interference, we have limits and will stop our children from mutual destruction.

You are too valuable in the grand design of existence and while you may not value yourselves, like parents we know how precious you are and do what we must to preserve our investment of love, time and energy.

Thus begins the era of disclosure. While the passing of time feels different for you, for us things move quite rapidly and now they accelerate.

I hope you enjoy my story for it is a human/alien/Anunnaki story that explains much while continuing the mystery. For even as old and as wise part of myself is, the human part remains human and as such there's much I don't know. As a third dimensional being I too must sit back and watch all unfold in divine fashion as we are all, God and mortal alike a part of the grand experiment designed by the Creator of All which is the totality of us and we are all part of that totality.

Janet Kira Lessin ~ Bio

Janet is an author (http://www.amazon.com/author/janetkiralessin), educator, experiencer, contactee, researcher, conference presenter, conference organizer, radio show host, workshop leader and counselor. She and her husband, Dr. Sasha Lessin, facilitate experiencers at conferences, in skype groups and in their growth center in Maui, Hawaii. She works with those who channel, who engage in shamanic journeywork, or who use tantric ritual to access the superconscious.

Likewise, her specialties include tarrying with those who experience abduction, astral contact or paranormal activity, who belong to alien contact groups, or who have supernormal and nature guides. Janet's practice encompasses those who access the dead, experienced near death experiences, who get powerful psychic intimations, who experience themselves and others as multidimensional. In her practice, Janet helps ground those in contact with the metacosmic void.

Janet presents PowerPoints based on her life as an Experiencer (which began at birth), plus information based on her research which includes presentations based on the Anunnaki, ancient aliens, Ufology, Experiencers and her work as a counselor with Dr. Sasha Lessin dealing with clients who've experienced paranormal and ET contact plus non-ordinary states of consciousness (such as astral travel, remote viewing, shamanic journeys, etc.).

Janet presents solo or with her beloved husband, Dr. Sasha Lessin. Janet and Sasha love to present together. Together they facilitate workshops, experiencer groups and private counseling sessions. Sessions, workshops and educational tutorials are based on the Anunnaki, ancient aliens, tantra, spiritual emergence, relationship counseling, life coaching, personal growth counseling, kundalini awakening and more.

At 13, saddened with the hypocrisy of religion, Janet embarked on a spiritual path–read hundreds of books on the paranormal, psychology and consciousness expansion and, in seminars and counseling, overcame her childhood abuse issues and learned to help others.

In 1997, Janet wed Dr. Sasha Lessin and began teaching with him. In their work with experiencers, contactees and psychics, the Lessins adapt methods from Holotropic Breathwork, Existential Analysis, Tantra, Voice Dialogue, Gestalt, Hypnotherapy, Past and Future Life Regression and Progression as well as Imago Work. They teach experiencers how to center themselves and integrate the energies they access in extraterrestrial and inter-dimensional, as well as paranormal experiences.

Janet is the author of "Dance of the Souls: Pierce the Veil" Janet is the co-author of "Anunnaki: Legacy of the Gods & Anunnaki: False Gods."

Janet Kira and Dr. Sasha Lessin
1371 Malaihi Road, Wailuku, HI 96793
808-244-4103

The Lessins teach and employ hypnosis, Jungian Past life Therapy, Holotropic Breathworker, Yoga, Tantra, Spirit Releasement, Extraterrestrial and exopolitical deprogramming, Voice Dialogue Centering, Existential Analysis, Gestalt Therapy, Spiritual growth and Psychosynthesis.

Websites:
www.schoolofcounseling.org
www.extraterrestrialcontact.com
www.enkispeaks.com
www.schooloftantra.com
www.worldpolyamoryassociation.com
www.worldpeaceassociation.com
www.ninmah.com
www.experiencersnetwork.com
www.aliencontactorganization.com
www.aquarianradio.com

We also have many related pages and groups on Facebook and other social networks on counseling, spirituality, tantra, relationship choice, extraterrestrial and paranormal contact. The Lessins specialize in clearing intensives, facilitated regression, progression and shamanic journeywork.

The Lessins are available for in-person, phone or skype sessions.

Email:
sashalessinphd@aol.com, janetlessin@gmail.com
808-244-4103 or 808-214-3442

BENEFIT FROM EXTRATERRESTRIAL CONTACT

Sasha Alex Lessin, Ph.D.

(Dean, School of Counseling, Certified Hypnotherapist)

WE'VE HAD ET CONTACT FROM THE GETGO

Extraterrestrials have interacted with us, the current Earthlings, since 300,000 years ago, when geneticists of the Goldmining Expedition from Planet Nibiru to Earth (the Anunnaki) adapted (adding Proto-Sasquatch genes, copper, minerals and mDNA) their genome to this planet to create us as their slave race. Statues, clay tablets and oral traditions tell us many a story of our ancestors traveling in and viewing Nibiran spacecraft.

Ancient Sumerian depiction of rocket in silo, astronauts within

Ancient depiction of Mayan Astronaut in rocket

We see ETs' skeletons, advanced technological devices, models of their aircraft, depictions of their astronauts and megalithic structures on every continent, under the seas and in the caverns deep within the Earth.

The wall at Pumapunku, Peru next to their spaceport at Tiahuancu features reliefs of Greys and Cone heads.

The Bible abounds with stories of ETs intervening in the affairs of Earthlings.

Elijah rockets to Nibiru

Modern UFO research and documented contactee testimonies give us evidence that any reasonable court of law would find utterly convincing that we have been and still are in extensive contact with ETs and that the Nations of Earth have made treaties of cooperation with Extraterrestrials, some of whom have abducted Earthlings for experimentation, breeding and slavery.

Millions of people from every continent have been in direct, personal and astral contact with ETs on this and other planets, in space and on their craft.

Contemporary Earth governments and the Vatican have

suppressed information about their clandestine treaties and ridiculed, intimidated, ruined and even assassinated people who have blown the whistle on our leaders' agreements with the ETs as well as our secret space program bases and orbiting craft as well as those of several species of extraterrestrials on Mars, Luna and other planets and satellites in our solar system and others.

GET A NONJUDGMENTAL HYPNOTHERAPIST

If you want to explore Alien contact you may have had, get a nonjudgmental, open hypnotherapist. This person shows you how to accept yourself, your subselves, and your experiences.

She or he hears what you say you experience and doesn't bug you about whether what you saw, felt, heard, intuited, and envisioned was real. Your therapist says, *"After the trance session, you'll remember of the session what's in your best interest to remember when the time's right for you to remember it."*

You came to hypnosis to explore alien contact, but past, future, parallel or interdimensional lives may flood your consciousness. You may well then relive ET contact you had in these incarnations in other bodies, times and places.

Trance-work lets you recall way more detail of how you

and aliens contacted each other.

Again, though you came to explore your alien experiences, you may instead relive military or cult abductions, psychedelic journeys, vision quests or astral trips. The alien memories you access can, in your trance, segue with womb, childhood and adult memories. Whatever you notice, your therapist helps you drop fear, trauma and memory blocks when it serves you to do so.

Perhaps you'll hear again words and thoughts you and your hybrid kids and ancestors shared as you and they dwelt in other bodies, times and places–within the Earth, in space on spacecraft, on other planets and in nonphysical realms.

You could remember sex with aliens or merge with the Creator-of-All.

You benefit from the perspectives and wisdom you gain during the contact and when you expand your memories in trance you get even more benefits. Inevitably, you give the world the insights you got, still get and will continue to get from alien contact.

Your therapist lets you recall alien contacts at a pace you can assimilate. In trance, you can keep enlarging what you recall. You glean more details.

You see how you and your family members have made ET contact all your lives.

You see that contact's ongoing and will probably continue.

You get that you consented to alien contact.

You celebrate your mission in the Big Story.

You end each hypnotherapy session when you've had enough for now; your therapist won't push you. She or he helps you center yourself so you can operate in daily life, honor your ecology and recognize, accept and address the needs of your Inner Child, Internal Critic, Social Subself and Inner Therapist.

CONTACT CLUES

The great alien contact hypnotherapist, Barbara Lamb, says that how you react to alien contact "may range from wonder, awe, and enlightenment to extreme anxiety, phobias, and sometimes, inability to function."

Mysterious interruptions in your life, disorientation, confusion, panic attacks, anxieties you don't understand, flashbacks, intense dreams, fears that you're crazy, distrust of others, addiction, compulsions, psychic abilities, fears of being left alone or fears bright lights follow you may be clues aliens contacted you. If you fear darkness, if you're scared of falling asleep, these fears may lead you in therapy, to a repressed ET contact memory.

Lamb writes that if you fear praying mantises, spiders, snakes or worry about animal or owl eyes your hypnotist can use these fears as gateways to recall alien contacts you repressed.

Here's more hints you had alien contact: you sleep clothed, wake at a certain time each night, feel like you've been dropped into bed, wake in strange positions, waken in rooms other than the one in which you went to sleep or wake miles away from your house, or wake up with your clothes on backward or not waken wearing clothes that belong to someone else.

Suspect alien contact if you have scoop-shaped scars, triangular marks on your butt, pus in your navel, fingertip marks on your body, pin-prick marks, lumps near your ear on or on your forehead.

Headaches, pains behind an eye, stiffness, back, neck or genital pain, nose problems, ringing or buzzing in your ears or blood on your pillow may, when you enter a trance, flash you back to an alien contact.

If you carried a fetus but hadn't had sex, if you had a

fetus in your uterus for a few months and then that fetus vanished without a trace, you probably had contact with ETs and should explore this with your therapist.

FREQUENT ALIEN MEMORIES

When you relive alien contact, you may feel again paralysis, you may re-experience levitating, moving through walls and windows, remember beaming up You might recall ETs on a spacecraft doing medical procedures on you or re-experience ambassador tutorials with ETs, or training classes you had on a spacecraft with other children who have become people in your life now.

Whatever you recall, hypnotherapy can help you "assimilate and make sense of bizarre experiences and function well, even though these experiences continue."

ALIENS TOLD YOU TO FORGET

Your therapist helps you relive alien contacts and to see the resonances of the alien experiences in ever-expanding detail even if aliens told you to forget them. You recorded everything you saw, felt, heard and thought. All your experiences imprinted in your biocomputer's memory banks, some of which has been offline in your unconscious.

You can, with hypnotherapy, relive your experiences and

release emotions and thoughts from your alien contacts. You learn to use your memories to better your life and enjoy ongoing contacts with the aliens.

"You have a right," Lamb says, "to know. No harm will come to you or the aliens by remembering and sharing."

ACCESS EXTRATERRESTRIALS THOUGH YOUR CENTER

If you're an extraterrestrial or interdimensional Contactor, you may've suppressed an inner voice that agreed to your contacts. Perhaps you agreed and forgot you did.

Maybe you remember ETs invaded you and think they did so against your will. But a protective part of you– a primary subself–labeled the contact to which you agreed as "involuntary." Your primary self may have hidden from your awareness that you said yes to paranormal or extraterrestrial contact.

Sometimes after extensive therapy and maturity you realize a part of you–a suppressed subpersonality, alter, part or repressed inner voice–did say "yes' to contact. Your social or primary subselves can push your Inner Contactor, a voice inside your head–from your conscious awareness to shield you from conventional people who'd shame, punish, or even lock you away for recalling and speaking of your ET or other paranormal experiences.

But it can be safe now to let yourself to experience part of you that wants you to remember your experiences with ghosts, spacefaring entities, time travelers, and spirit guides as well as your own existence on other planets, in other dimensions and in the past and future.

To the degree that you judge it safe, you can remember and even judiciously share your experiences with other Contactors as well as people in the ET-experiencers' networks. You can, of course, share under a pen name and keep your privacy.

I suggest you let yourself remember such experiences. You can opt to keep your contacts private or share them. You learn, when you follow the cues below, to review and relive your contacts from your Center. Then you choose what to tell and what to hide from those who might freak if they hear what you experienced.

The cues teach you to center yourself, to identify with your Center. Your Center is your conscious awareness of your many subselves or inner voices. From your ever-expanding Center, you coordinate behavior that meets the deep needs of ever more of your inner voices. Your Center takes into account the needs of your Contactor subself as well as the needs of your primary social and practical selves. Primary selves like your Pleaser,

Intellect, Parent, Judge and Self-Critic may keep you from the full awareness of the Contactor part of you so you can meet your social duties and not sound like a crazy to other people.

From your Center, you choose the degree to which you reveal or conceal your Contactor subself and its unconventional experiences. You assess how much of your Contactor you reveal to your own awareness and to other people.

From your Center you can assess probable pushback you'll get if you remember and share your contacts. You predict possible pushback from mates, friends, bosses, disinformation agents, military intimidators, religious bigots, and people who fear your revelations.

Such people may fear your revelations if they've repressed their own paranormal intimations. You decide how much to reveal and how much to conceal, but you can at least let yourself remember.

The cue sequence below begins with an evocation of your primary inner voices. Seek their permission to explore your Contactor. Your primary voices that protect you from shame and punishment may've blocked you from either recalling your contacts or may have blocked you from recalling that you consented to contact.

You must get permission from your protective primary voices to let you hear the memories, desires and needs of your Inner Contactor. In the cue-sequence, you tell your primary voices you'll let them stop interviewing your Contactor if these they sense that you're recalling too much too fast. Your protective voices let you remember enough for you to handle as you respond to the cues to follow.

CREATE PRIVATE SETTING WHERE YOU CAN EMOTE LOUDLY

Disconnect phone, make sure no one can interrupt you for a few hours as you work through the cues. You'll need several chairs or cushions and an area large enough area to lie down. Wear loose-fitting clothes. Create semi-darkness in the room.

VET A CUE-READER OR EXPLORE IN PRIVATE

Ask a nonjudgmental friend or therapist–your Reader–to read the cues to you. Tell her or him to give you plenty of time–at least five deep breaths–to respond to each cue. Make sure the reader doesn't challenge the reality status (ontology) of your contact memories or ask questions that imply answers s/he expects.

If you lack an open-minded reader, read the cues aloud into a recording device and play them to yourself. Or read each cue to yourself and take as much time as you like to respond aloud or in writing.

[*Instructions for Reader*]

*Read the cues in **bold** aloud to the experiencer. Exception: read words in square brackets* [like this] *silently. The person to whom you read is "the Experiencer."*

Give the experiencer a few breaths' time to respond aloud where you see asterisks (***). If the experiencer doesn't respond to a cue-sentence, pause several breaths and read the cue aloud again.

Address the Experiencer's inner voices and the entities s/he invokes respectfully, appreciatively; do not push their limits. Start now; read aloud:

CUES

[*Center Yourself*]

Sit here [Indicate place]; **it's the place for you to center yourself where you hear all your inner voices (parts). I'll address your Center with your name** [example: "Alex" is the name of my Center].

Breathe deeply and center yourself.

Tell me, Center, about one of the main protective

inner voices (like Intellect, Critic, Pleaser, and Pusher) you present to the world. What words or labels do you use for that voice?** [Example: I call my Primary "Professor Lessin"]

Describe this primary voice, the one you call [Use the same word Experiencer did to label the Primary]**. Say what this Primary's like and what it does for you. *****

Thank you, Center.

[Identify with a Primary Subself]

Disidentify with your Center and move to a new place to embody this Primary--a subself from which you relate to other people.

[Wait till Experiencer moves. when you read the cues, substitute the name (e.g.: Inner Critic) with which Experiencer "Primary" where you see the word "Primary" below].

Hi. Embody that Primary. Say who you are [in example, you'd say, *"Embody your Critic and say who you are."*] **and the job you do in your Experiencer's ecology. *****

When, Primary, did your life start? How long have you been around? What's your history as [Experiencer name] **'s Primary? *****

Say, Primary, what voices you protect? ***

What contributions have you, as [Experiencer name]**'s Primary, made to** [Experiencer's name] **throughout life?** ***

What would you like to be acknowledged and appreciated for? ***

When I'll ask you, Primary, to let [Experiencer's name] **speak from an inner voice that accesses ETs, ghosts, multidimensionals, visions, dreams and/or simultaneous existences in other times and places, if you sense your person's Inner Child panic, shift the Contactor voice offstage and again take center-stage in Experiencer's consciousness.**

Thank you, Primary. I liked talking with you. Now let [Experiencer's name] **return to the Center position.**

[*Return to Center*]

[Wait till Experiencer moves.] **Hello again, Center. Say what you learned about the primary voice you just embodied.** ***

Tell me, Center, about your Contactor--an inner subself–that experiences the paranormal. ***

Move your seat to a new place for your Contactor.

[*Embody Contactor*]

[Wait till Experiencer moves.] **Become your Contactor. As Contactor, say what name your person can call you** ***

[Example: what I call my contactor "Alexander-Ben-Irving." use Experiencer's name for the word "Contractor" wherever you see it in the cues].

Say, Contactor, how you are, what you do for [Experiencer's name] **and what you like.** ***

[*Contact Events*]

Tell me, Contactor, and main contact events with ETs, ghosts, multidimensionals, visions, dreams and/or simultaneous existences in other times and places in this and other lives with [Experiencer's name]. ***

Relate one critical contact event in this life, a past life or future life. ***

[*Trance Induction Steps*]

Imagine, contactor, you descend ten steps a spiral

stairway. Each time you exhale, slide your hand along the bannister, go down a step and relax more. [Pause] after a while, step off of the staircase and onto a landing.

See a blackboard and chalk on the landing. Take the chalk and write a number on the blackboard corresponding to how relaxed you are. 1-12 is slightly relaxed; 13-24, moderately; 25+, very relaxed. Tell me the number you write on the blackboard. ***

Relax more by writing the succeeding number below the first one. Relax still more by writing the next number behind the first one. Write the next number above your initial number, and relax more. Deepen your relaxation: write the next number in front of the first one. What number do you write in front? ***

[*Elevator-Transporter*]

Opposite the blackboard, see an elevator which is also a transporter. Its dial shows you're on a floor, numbered the same as how many years old you are now. Enter the elevator-transporter.

Push one of the elevator buttons. the floor number on the button you push is the year to which you'll descend to access a critical event that might make your person's contact experiences more accessible to conscious awareness. What's the number on the button you pushed? ***

Go down in the elevator to the floor/age of the button you pushed. If your person experienced the event in a past life, let the elevator go to the subterranean floors of the building. If s/he experienced the event in a parallel or dream world existence, let him or her enters the transporter chamber under the building, activate the transporter, and emerge in the alternate reality.

[*Relive Critical Contact Experience*]

Emerge from the elevator or *transporter* and step into a hall. There, see many doors. One bears your name and the contact experience that will help you remember so your Center can access your contacts.

Open the door to your critical contact experience. Go inside a *holographic chamber* that can let you relive the experience. Any time, you can shift to a neutral, witnessing mode, detached from emotion or you can let a primary subself take you from this reverie if it is too intense for you right now.

See, hear, feel, sense and intuit everyone and everything as it was when you first experienced it.

Use the present (is, am, are) tense and describe the contact you relive. Experience and tell me in detail:

What you see ****

What you hear ****

What you feel ****

What you smell ****

What you taste ****

What you sense ****

What you think ****

What you intuit ****

How do you breathe during this situation? ****

Do you get an implant, upgrade, pregnancy, healing during the experience. ****

Do you give ova, sperm or a fetus in the experience? ****

[*Speak as "Other" & Other's Commander*]

Now let "other" (one of the beings or people present or implied in the experience) speak with your voice, but not take you over. Temporarily identify with and vocalize for the "other" in your paranormal experience. [Allow plenty of time–take 10 breaths before you read the next cue].

Who are you, Being Who Will Speak with [Experiencer's name]**'s Voice?** ***

What are your *reasons* for contacting [Experiencer's name]**?** ***

What *mission* do you have for [Experiencer's name]? ***

How does your contact with [Experiencer's name] **fit into a *program* you're working?** ***

Why did you *implant, upgrade or manipulate* the Contactee's reproductive material and organs? ***

What's your existence and the existence of your colleagues like in space, time, on your *Homeworld*, or in your *dimension*? ***

How is your Homeworld *organized*? How is it organized politically? ***

Describe housing, family and social relations on your

Homeworld. Tell me about transport devices and craft there. ***

Cross-connect with your headquarters. We wish to speak with your *High Commander*. [Allow time]

Commander, tell us through your subordinate who now speaks through my Experiencer's voice, what your purpose is in contacting my Experiencer. ***

What mission do you have for contactors in general and for my Experience in particular? ***

Thank you, Commander. Now let your subordinate– the one we're calling "Other"– resume speaking through [Experiencer's name]**'s voice.**

As the voice of the "Other", what else would you like your person to know before you release her/his voice? ***

Thank you, "Other."

[*Embody contactor again*]

Return again to the seat for your Contactor.

[Wait till Experiencer moves back to the place where s/he enacts Contactor]

Hello again, Contactor. Tell your person what you'd like to be appreciated for now and through the years. ***

What do you want, Contactor? ***

Why do you want that? What needs motivate what you want? ***

What else would you like your person to know before s/he goes back to Center? ***

Bid adieu to your Contactor for now. Exit the holo room, return to the elevator-transporter in the building of your ages. Go back in the elevator-transporter to the floor of your current age.

Go past the blackboard where you chalked the numbers, then ascend the stairs that lead you back to right here. On the tenth steps from the top, feel your consciousness start to return to the present. Step 9, more awake. 8,7,6, 5, becoming more awake. 4, 3, 2– almost totally alert. 1–wake up, fully awake and alert

[Snap your fingers; give Experiencer time to re-orient.]

[*Return to Center*]

Welcome back. Move back to the place for your Center. [Wait till s/he moves]

As Center, what did you learn from accessing your contactor and the voice of the "other" and its commander that your paranormal voice channeled for you? ***

[*Identify with Neutral Witness*]

Stand behind me and become neutral. Witness the energy from each of the positions–the Primary's, Contactor's, and other voices' seats–from which you spoke as I summarize what each said. Feel the energy of each as I review them for you.

[Synopsize what Experiencer said from each voice]. ###

[*Return to Center*]

Experience yourself between your Primary and your Contactor. With the info from your Witness on your current ecology, regulate how much of your Contactor's experience to reveal and what to conceal in various social contexts. Comment on the balance that seems right for you now. ***

[*Own Your Power*]

Pull your energy back from me; realize you now know

how to conduct this sort of exploration on your own, without my reading to you.

References

Lamb, B., 2016, "Extra-Terrestrial Contact Experiences: How Regression Therapy Can Help", the Journal of Regression Therapy

Lessin, S. and J.
1998 – present, extraterrestrialcontact.com

Stone, H. & Winkelman, S.,
1998, "Embracing Our Selves", and "Embracing Each Other" both 1989, New World Library: San Rafael).

Sasha Alex Lessin, Ph.D. ~ Bio

Sasha Lessin has a Ph.D. and an M.A. in Anthropology (U.C.L.A.) and a Master's in Counseling Psychology (University for Humanistic Studies). He studied the Anunnaki--giant people from the planet Nibiru who created us--under Zecharia Sitchin, and, with Sitchin's encouragement, co-wrote Anunnaki: Gods No More (2012), Legacy of The Gods (2014) and Anunnaki False Gods (2015) with wife Janet.

Dr. Lessin is also a Certified Hypnotherapist specializing in Experiencer/Contactee memory expansion. "We teach each experiencer to witness and center herself. She learns to embrace the parts of her (subselves) that--consciously or not--consents to paranormal, extraterrestrial and/or interdimensional contact. She accesses, dialogues with and coordinate needs of her other subpersonalities--her Inner Child, Social Persona, Critic, Professional subself, etc--with needs her Contactor seeks to meet in ET or paranormal contact.

TRUTH BE TOLD: I AM AN EXPERIENCER

Karen Christine Patrick

*Book Cover: The Anunnaki and the Moon
book available at www.sheppardandpatrick.com*

RECRUITMENT

Karen Christine Patrick - Experiencer

My name is Karen Christine Patrick. I am an experiencer. Primarily, I have been a contactee. What that means is that I have experienced telepathic contact with extraterrestrial beings, ancestors, ghosts, inter-dimensional beings, and other intelligences. Also, I am a host on Aquarian Radio and an "admin" for the Facebook group the "Lunar Anomaly Research Society" studying anomalies on the moon and the Apollo missions stories.

Links:

LUNAR ANOMALY RESEARCH SOCIETY - facebook.com/groups/LARS.PUBLIC/

AQUARIAN RADIO - https://www.aquarianradio.com

One of my contact experiences has been making contact with the Anunnaki, a race that has been part of humanity's story from antiquity. In those ancient alien tales, it is said they had bases on the moon. Also, "anomalists," those who study anomalies in space agency photos, say they have seen modern structures in lunar images as well. Despite the attempts to hide these facts, photographic and other evidence indicates there is more to the story. I can only share my own experiences, I leave it to the reader to decide. Personally, I find these tantalizing stories fascinating and I want to share what I've been looking into with others.

PROJECT TALENT

In 1968, I was 7 years old. I was in the first grade in the California school system and I was in the testing process to be a part of "Project Talent." After these tests, I was put into the Gifted and Talented program. "Project Talent" stated that they were looking for gifted kids to track towards college, but behind the scenes, they were looking for kids with psi talent, intuitives, who were also highly compliant, or could be made to be so.

EXPERIENCERS CONSCIOUS CONTACTEES

Project Talent sought Psi-gifted kids

My parents took me out of the program after I was sent to the Vice Principal's office and a man who was not part of the school staff gave me a full psychological profile without their knowledge. Strangely, he had me play a "guessing game" using something called "Zener Cards,"

ZENER CARDS for testing ESP/Psi talent

used to test for ESP. When my parents found out, they took me out of the public school and put me into a religious school.

Later, I found that kids from Project Talent were put into various programs, including super-soldier programs, psychic-warfare programs, remote viewing programs, and even to be used to communication with all kinds of beings.

In the last number of years, I have met many of these "program kids" who often became adults with PTSD, Dissociative Disorder, and with other trauma- based effects.

Many of these program kids, now grown up, are remembering more and more of their experiences and are speaking out. I admire the power of the human spirit to overcome adversity in those who tell their story.

A pattern also seems to be that contactees like myself are also "program kids." This program is quite vast as the United States pursued a permanent war economy. The current iteration of program kids seem to be involved in an advancement of technologies into a concept called "Transhumanism."

Link:
http://www.bibliotecapleyades.net/sociopolitica/sociopol_mindconMKULTRA03.htm

PAPERCLIP, MK ULTRA, & MONARCH

From my research, I think that Project Talent is one of the many programs spawned from something called

"Project Paperclip" that brought Nazi scientists into America after World War II and going into the Cold War era. Some of the Nazi scientists were researching trauma-based mind control, experimenting on people in concentration camps using drugs and torture, before being brought over to the United States. When the program studying mind control was set up in the US, it was called MK-ULTRA with MK standing for "Mind Kontrol," where the word "Kontrol" is the German spelling for Control.

Project Paperclip German Scientists, Fort Bliss, Texas

These secret programs proliferated into more "Projects" studying different kinds of mind control techniques, being developed as a response to perceived threats from the Russian and Chinese communists. One of the kids I met in my Project Talent class was a victim in a program using sexual molestation trauma as a part of its mind-control techniques. This program was called "Project Monarch." When I was slipping out of the grasp of the teachers, when my parents took me out of the public school, I was befriended by this student, who happened to be a neighbor kid who was used to be my best friend and also "watch" me.

*Link:
http://www.bibliotecapleyades.net/sociopolitica/sociopol_mindconMKULTRA.htm#contents*

One thing that I still don't understand is why she told me of her trauma, in horrific detail. I thought these kids blocked out the trauma. She was telling me things no grade school child should know anything about. I think she was prompted by her controllers to do this as part of the recruitment process. Maybe it was the idea of having a secret together, creating a bond, or if I became too curious, it would be as if I were giving permission to be abused. I was glad when we moved away, out of California, just at that time.

MAKING CONTACT

A.R. Bordon of the Life Physics Group

A.R. Bordon of the Life Physics Group and the Linkage Institute

A.R.BORDON was the pen name, likely, of a very peculiar, but fascinating mentor I had along the way. If ever the statement was true for me, "When the student is ready, the teacher appears" it was in my interaction with A.R. Bordon.

Bordon's story was that he was a renegade physicist in the "black" or secret world and that he disagreed that the findings of his group should keep the secrets they discovered from the public. This group, the "Life Physics Group" had information Bordon thought should not be held back from the rest of humanity. As evidence of his story, he released some fascinating writings that I am still studying.

The Life Physics Group scientists partnered with "intuitives" to "remote view" the "implicate order" scientist David Bohm talked about, which could be defined as the energetic substructure of manifest reality. This topic is taboo in conventional circles, therefore the scientists in the Life Physics Group used pseudonyms in the writings.

The result of this collaboration between scientists and psychics was a working model called "Ideomaterial Physics." The part of the word "Ideo" means ideas or thought becoming "material" things manifesting in our reality. There is strong correlation between the Quantum

Hologram theory and Ideomaterial Physics. Bordon passed away in 2013 and I created a Facebook group called, "The Writings of AR Bordon" to file share files with the many friends I made through Bordon.

Link:
https://www.facebook.com/groups/writingsofarbordon/

A.R. Bordon was the one who confirmed for me my early recruitment in Project Talent, about the existence of other secret programs, plus he confirmed my ability to contact beings and to utilize a human psychic capacity called "Extension Neurosensing." This is similar to remote viewing, but can include all the senses, not just "viewing."

IDEOMATERIAL PHYSICS

A.R. Bordon introducing me to "Ideomaterial Physics," an alternative to the Standard Model, was an expansive concept making room for what we call "paranormal" abilities. It is my belief that the internet was "sold" by the ETs to the "powers-that-be" to be a control-grid over the population of the planet, but actually is "thoughtform" technology to show us how information exists in its "natural habitat," in the realm of various levels of consciousness. What we call "cyberspace," or the mental virtual reality called "The Cloud" mimics something AR Bordon called "The Cumulus" which is all the shared information of a collective, such as any biological species. Researcher Rupert Sheldrake called this the "morphogenetic field."

This morphogenetic field, sometimes called the "biokind biomind," is used to gather all the information a species needs from the life experiences of each individual, to be able to adapt to changes in the environment and improve its chances of survivability. I learned from A.R. Bordon about aspects of "Idiomaterial Physics" that he and the Life Physics Group were working on, the attempt to articulate a cosmological paradigm that is energy-, rather than particle-based.

The morphogenetic field is studied as part of the investigation of the of "ideomaterial" construct, with "ideo" referring to "information, thought, or ideas," and "material" is referring to the "manifestation of matter" in the medium of consciousness. An applicable spiritual principle expressing this idea is, "In (the consciousness of God) we live and move and have our being."

Link: http://tinyurl.com/IDEOMATERIAL-PHYSICS-Essay-One

AN INTRODUCTORY SUMMARY OF WHAT IDIOMATERIAL PHYSICS IS BY THE AUTHORS:

"The Life Physics Group—California (LPG-C) has been engaged in discoveries about space/time ratios beyond the fractal fuzzy boundaries of the known universe. These space/time ratios have been labeled the Unum because of their unique inter-connectivity and characteristics.

Book: Ideomaterial Physics by A.R. Bordon

LPG-C has been working to uncover the secrets of Nature through the use of extension neurosensing (ENS), a technology array that involves the stabilization of human neurophysiologic processes to allow the biomind (or body/mind) the freedom of immanent (internal) movement to move space-like (in time) or time-like (in space ratios) opening the doors of perception for mankind to explore the Universe and beyond in ways never before thought possible.

Information gathered through the use of this technology has not been easy to process and has taken neurosensors (LPG-C members) over a decade to decode and decipher multidimensional information into a comprehensible and emergent picture. It is this picture that has come to be known as the Working Model. This essay will report an outline of this basic Working Model and explore the foundational concepts and principles developed since the year 2000, the result being a magnificently complex and intelligent domain of interconnected thought and matter in an idiomaterial universe/Unum.

THE CONSCIOUNESS TREE

Since the entire cosmos is contained in the quantum hologram, which is manifesting in the medium of consciousness, all intelligences and beings are interconnected. It is through this inter-connectedness that telepathic and tel-empathic contact with our "invisible friends" is made possible. I differentiate between "telepathic" as being information-based and "telempathic" as being more feelings-based.

I call this tree-structure of communication "The Consciousness Tree." I tend to believe, though it is not necessarily always true, that making contact means that the information is important to the receiver in some way, that it is meant for guidance and understanding. Often, when one becomes more acquainted with a being from elsewhere, perhaps even becoming "friends" with a being, then there are conversations that are more "shoot the breeze" type of experiences. It can be a similar experience to making friends in social media.

Usually, this kind of contact is rendered as dangerous in some way, by religious beliefs that demonize the idea of this communication or by mainstream science to be some form of mental defect, but it is the results and nature of the information to be discerned, not just the way that it has come about. Those negatively disposed to this kind of contact will be highly skeptical in this methodology for receiving information, but tend to lack objectivity when hearing information from sources in the hierarchical leadership caste of their belief systems.

INVISIBLE FRIENDS

The most significant contact experiences that I will talk about in this section include:

UFO sighting in 1979, in Salem, Oregon along with a family member seeing a UFO go over us parallel to the highway we were on.

Automatic writing CONTACT telepathic "downloads" journaling and artistic sessions with a group of beings called, "All Guides" starting in November 2009 to the present day.

A contactee experience starting in 2011 with an Anunnaki ancestor which started me on the path to study the Anunnaki.

Contact with a greenish Grey calling himself Mr. Green, who says he is on the moon on a base on the far side, that he calls Luna Base.

UFO SIGHTING IN 1979

In 1979, my family and I were visiting a relative who was a locksmith in Salem, Oregon and I was helping in the shop, making keys. My godparent, Sid, got a call from a man who broke his key in the ignition of his car, so I was a ride-along in the locksmith van. We got to the restaurant where the car was parked and left after the keys were finished.

On our way back, it was about 8pm, a late dusky sunset because it was summer, and we were traveling West, towards the setting sun. On the horizon, we saw what looked like an airplane on fire, with orange-pink bright lights that were very bright. Sid stopped the van, concerned that the plane would try to land in the highway we were traveling on. I remember he turned off the ignition of the van and put the keys in his pocket as we stepped out to see what was going on.

UFO Sighting, 1979

An object came towards us that was not like anything we had ever seen before, the shape was a "star-tetrahedron" shaped. It had a glow in the middle and pink lights on all the points of the star tetrahedron shape. It moved across the sky rather low, at the height of a small airplane about to land, but was going much faster. It was aerodynamically impossible to be flying as we knew the properties of objects that fly, and it was completely silent as it traversed the sky.

AUTOMATIC WRITING CONTACT TELEPATHIC "DOWNLOADS" JOURNALING

Starting in 2009, I began a fascinating process that has set the agenda for my activities ever since. I have been journaling for quite a few years. It's part of my self-help regime. I was living on a boat at the time, and I think that is an important point because the positive energies of living intimately with nature became a healing experience for me. I began to transcribe something I now call "Transmissions from ALLGUIDES." These were beings who were able to transition through the growing pains Earth-based humans are going through now.

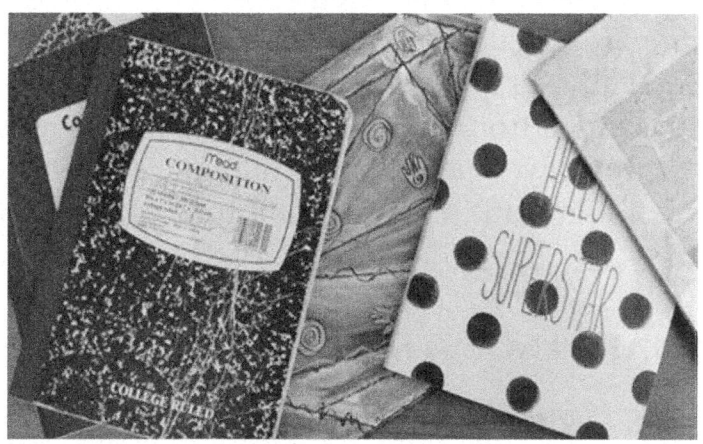

CONTACT Journaling and Art 2009 till present day

I learned a lot about belief systems and how different ET species organize their societies in a positive, benevolent, mature configuration. A few important points I learned from ALLGUIDES are that:

- Humanity is about to achieve the start of "Paradigm Galactic" which is an awareness that our planet exists in a populated cosmos.
- A collective of beings co-creates a shared reality through the energy of attention.
- Some advanced beings know about this co-creational aspect and used this knowledge to rule humans

through capturing attention through Theatrics, "Theo tricks," the Tricks of the "gods."
- We absolutely are being "upgraded" from a hierarchical, "fractional," scarcity-based system of human provisioning to a "holarchy" which is a "fractal" system based on creating abundance.
- Our current system is based on "compartmentalization" (come apart [with me] mental ally, I say shun [the others]) which keeps us all separated from each other but we will be applying, as the remedy, "integration" (into grace/gratitude - grace for human frailty and gratitude as a connecting force.

ANUNNAKI ANCESTOR

I met Godi Godesh when doing "spirit singing" which is an ad-lib kind of toning and singing the full capacity of one's range. It's a good meditation and warm-up for a singer. I was driving my car when this event happened, enjoying how the windshield reflected back my voice so I could hear it better. Suddenly, I felt the impetus to drop down into the lower part of my range, a the a low voice came out, "I Am Godi Godesh." I had made a connection, I later surmised, with an Anunnaki Ancestor through that Consciousness Tree I spoke of earlier. Afterwards, I spent quite a bit of time trying to discern the motivation of this being which I finally deemed as having positive intentions.

EXPERIENCERS CONSCIOUS CONTACTEES

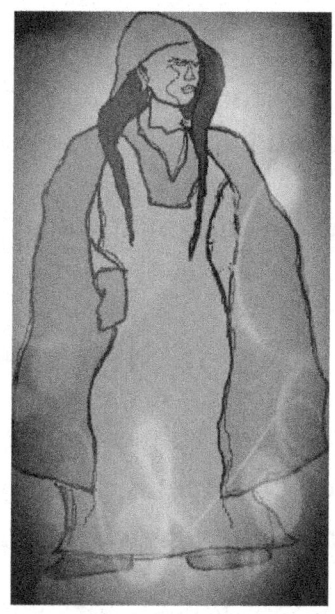

Godi Godesh, 12 ft. Anunnaki Ancestor contact

One caution given to me by A.R. Bordon that when dealing with telepathic contact with ET beings was to take off imaginary "WOW Goggles." I interpreted this advice meant to avoid being too overwhelmed by the contact and to use every means to validate what I am hearing through research and discernment.

This being:

- Called himself "Godi Godesh"
- Identified as an Anunnaki ancestor
- Claims he is a convert to the "pro-human-independence" Anunnaki Faction. (there are several factions in that collective)

- Sees the "spark of the divine" in humans after dealing with them directly for a time
- Was 9 feet tall and had an adult-onset growth to 12 feet tall
- Was a "general" over human warrior in war games of the Anunnaki

"GODI GODESH" NAME MEANINGS

"GODI" - A goði or gothi (plural goðar) is the Old Norse term for a priest and chieftain. Gyðja signifies a priestess. ***Linki: ttps://en.wikipedia.org/wiki/GODI***

"GODESH" - Hebrew "qodesh," or "kadesh" - This verb literally means "to be set apart for a special purpose". A noun derived from this verb is qodesh, someone or something that is set apart for a special purpose. ***Link: http://www.mechanical-translation.org/mt/articles_s.html***

MR. GREEN AND THE CAMERA

Bret and I were in a deep research phase of lunar anomalies, when I had this vision where I suddenly felt the need to put my "POV" near the moon. I had learned to use the POV, my awareness, P.O.V. or "Point Of View," as a state of observation similar to "remote viewing" or what A.R. Bordon called, E.N.S. "Extension Neurosensing" where one seems actually "there" in the place using multiple senses besides just viewing.

Mr. Green works on Luna Base

I made contact with Mr. Green when he was holding a camera. It was if I was a tiny speck coming out of the camera eyepiece and seeing this giant eyeball of an alien. It was very startling to me and also the alien, who could feel my presence. I was staring into the giant eyeball of a being I would come to call "Mr. Green." Mr. Green does not have black eyes like a grey, but green eyes, with flecks of brown, blue and black.

Mr. Green's people are similar to greys, but are their own species and a colony of them lives on Luna Base on the Moon. My POV adjusted back and to the side so I could see the scene not quite so close. I saw this being holding a camera that seemed rigged to be hand-held when it wasn't supposed to me. Telepathically, I was told that aliens helped take pictures for us on the pre-Apollo missions to find a landing place for the Lunar Landers. Again, I when get this kind of information, in this manner, I use it as a data point for research.

The very next day after I made contact, Bret found an image of Mr. Green holding a camera on a NASA image: LO1, 1197_med, an image from LUNAR ORBITER ONE. An amazing confirmation because I had seen this being rather "up close and personal" and could scarcely imagine why he was holding a camera.

Mr. Green holding Camera in Lunar Image

I was told that aliens helped take pictures for us on the pre-Apollo missions to find a landing place for the Lunar Landers. I just use a message like this as a jumping-off point for research. There are some "plot-holes" in the NASA narrative that have been pointed out by many anomalists and other researchers. It's to the point where some people don't believe humans even went to the moon. Wouldn't that make sense, as a possibility, that our space missions were aided by ETs in order to help usher us into a space paradigm? This could be even more of a possibility due to the primitive nature of our technology during the Apollo mission era. Back then, when a young President Kennedy set our sight on the putting humans on the moon, the military mind and need for positive propaganda created the imperative that "Failure is not an option."

END EXCERPT

I hope you like this excerpt. Look for this full book on SheppardAndPatrick.com - the website I share with my anomalist research partner, Bret Colin Sheppard and also listen on Aquarian Radio for the Friday show "The Experiencer Path" on AquarianRadio.com.

I hope you like this excerpt. Look for this full book on SheppardAndPatrick.com and also listen on Aquarian Radio for the Friday Show "The Experiencer Path" on BlogTalkRadio.com/AquarianRadio and AquarianRadio.com.

Karen Christine Patrick ~ Bio

Karen Christine Patrick was in recruitment as a schoolchild in California in a program called Project Talent, in the late 1960's, that was looking for gifted and talented students. Descendant from Project Paperclip and MK-Ultra, Project Talent was a clandestine program developed as a way to secretly screen schoolchildren for psychic and remote-viewing abilities. Because her parents put her in a religions school and because of Karen's religious upbringing, this caused her to suppress gnosive abilities. Later in life, not only does she remember many incidents of receiving downloads from the morphogenetic field, but she comes into contact with several alien intelligences, including an Anunnaki ancestor, These guides help her throw off the suppression and she is able to know what she needs to know to help catalyze Paradigm Galactic, humanity knowing about a populated cosmos.

Patrick has authored a book, "The Anunnaki and the Moon" and works with others in radio, and in publishing books. Karen is a co-host on Aquarian Radio on "The Experiencer Path" on Friday Nights.

ONCE AND FUTURE ART
Bret Colin Sheppard

UNIVERSAL IDEAS

When asked where I came from, my reply is Indiana. The truth is, I know I came from the earth and the stars, our earth parents are the portals of life for the container. The enigmatic energy that we call life originates from the stars. We are all from space, whether that space is right in front of you or the space we are all floating in. That enigmatic energy is what many call "god" which is what we share with every living container on earth.

I had heard that the different races of humanity had come here in waves; perhaps that are true for many, how they feel. For me, it truly feels like I had been here before and my life is a reflection of that reality.

The things that interest me are the most universal of ideas:

Where we did we come from?

Do we have past lives?

What is "god" exactly?

Why did we come here if there was a choice?

What is our purpose?

Other ideas of interest were ancient writings, origin stories that not only tell us these about things, but also convey the feeling that we are not alone in the universe. I feel like my family is out there somewhere.

I have been searching for that space family since I was very young. Observing my earth family with universal awareness changed everything. I saw them walk around me, was generally a happy, bald baby but something felt different. I never felt like I completely belonged, the dilemma of many, I suppose. It was something deep that I couldn't quite put my finger on. I would find out, as I grew, that things were not simple. I had questions developing in my mind as I was growing up.

Life is everywhere, we are a part of it all. Our observations change things on the atomic level every day, a mystery on the quantum level. It is the observation that "observation changes things" meaning all may be an illusion. If so, none of us are in control of destiny.

My life has been a kaleidoscope of memories in displaced time, making it difficult to put into perspective the exact time frame of events. My story includes one event, so bizarre, that a dream scape would seem less fanciful. My life has been very surreal, how my art imitates my life. To my dyslexic mind, I would rather state that my life often my imitates art.

PICTURES IN THE DARK

My story begins with the young, impressionable boy that I was back in the 1970's. I was just about ten years old, by then I had been fiddling around with art as far back as I could remember, working in crayons, pencil... whatever was available.

I wasn't yet technically very good, but had an enormous amount of potential. This was the opinion of me, looking through the eyes of a woman that seems to have disappeared from this reality, I cannot find her anywhere in this age of the internet.

For me, she was a very real teacher, influential at a time when I was to be shown who I was, what I was able to do. I was to become a better artist because I was a very natural one. I saw shapes in just about everything that I looked... tiles in the bathroom, clouds, trees... you name it. Life looked like a dream scape to me because my dreams were real.

Her name was Ino, she was one of my mom's friends that my mom met in Chicago and brought back home from Mr. Kenny's bar. Ino was a cartoon artist working under Shel Silverstein and Phil Interlandi. She was a very gifted artist and her instruction was to me orientation into the world of fine art. She taught me some techniques to enhance my abilities and also taught me about some of the psychology in art. I would also say she taught me the fundamentals of what we call, "remote viewing" today.

When I was very young, I studied from instructional books by Walter Lanz, did a lot of sketching, teaching myself what I could. People and animals were my favorite subject matter. In regular school, I took art classes, further developing technical skills. Also developing right along was my perception, always a bit surreal. I remember one of my first art pieces, a drawing my mother referred to as the "orphan picture." It was an image of a very sad-looking Irish child, so compelling it was almost a bit creepy to look at, the face looking slightly distorted, it's eyes communicating as though it had lived a whole lifetime, ghost-like.

I was in High School, in the late fall of 1982, when I had an experience that was so strange, it haunted me for most of my life until just recently. I woke up that morning after a night of dreaming of creating art, looking forward to my art class, to the fun and camaraderie I experienced there.

I really had no idea that my strange day would change my life forever. I got through my usual classes, anticipating my art class and the projects I was working on. I remember I was working on a large clay pot on the ceramics wheel. I also was working on another one of my surreal drawings, one that was going to be in an art show later that year, to be adjudicated and displayed by the Daughters of Liberty organization.

While I was working on my drawing, I saw my art

teacher, Mr. Mikrut, talking to a dark-haired, exotic-looking woman named Ximena Zurita who appeared as a visitor to the class. I remember her name very clearly because when Mr. Mikrut introduced her to the class, he called her "noxema" instead of Ximena. This was his self-effacing way of making light of the difficulty he was having of pronouncing her name, something he often did to set his students at ease when learning their names.

Ms. Zurita said she was from the Stanford Research Institute and wanted to show a few of us some slides after class. Mr. Mikrut picked me and another student named Chris to be the ones to stay after class for a few hours to view the presentation.

There was something very odd about Ms. Zurita and the situation, I could feel that. I was feeling very strange anticipating the after school event.

The slide show began, utilizing a 1980's-era slide projector with the round racks to hold the individual slides. We were told that we would be shown some art by various artists and we were to offer feedback on what we saw in the images. The presentation seemed very strange to me. I felt that I had seen the images before but I didn't know where... they felt eerily familiar. The images were of people in costumes, dragons, Vikings, hound dogs, and other images. Some of the images were of an erotic nature which made me uncomfortable to view, it felt inappropriate to me, still a minor. She made light of that, acknowledging the discomfort. All the while looking at the images, I felt I had done this before, feeling a strong sense of Deja' vu.

When the lights came on and presentation was over, she asked us further what we thought about the images. I remember saying to her that they felt familiar during the presentation. I told her that a few images I commented on felt like they were from dreams I've had in the past. She gave no feedback about the images. She gave a sigh and thanked us for participating, adding "Have a great evening." She seemed disappointed. I didn't know what she wanted me to say. Ms. Zurita packed up her things asking Mr. Mikrut if she could speak to him in private.

As I went home, I thought that was all very strange. I felt much "singled out" and wondered, "Why me?" I didn't feel privileged, or that my artistic opinion was what was being evaluated, but something else. I just was left with a creepy feeling.

A PERSONAL DISCLOSURE

It is important to share my paranormal experiences at this point. That I believe that my art is connected with ET/ED extra-terrestrial, extra-dimensional communication is based on a significant set of experiences I've had over the years with such communication that did not particularly involve art. I believe part of my heritage as a person of Irish descent and part of my personal make up as a psychic intuitive and empath makes otherworldly communication "normal" for me.

My initial experience with ET/ED beings was not at all traumatic but rather beautiful. The beings were in my dreams and were there for me when black outs occurred from pain. I had a very abusive upbringing. They helped me cope by taking me out of my body so I didn't have to feel what was happening to me. What I learned later was that these experiences were not just my imagination, but rather a part of another reality that I couldn't see unless triggered or traumatized.

I would call them angels but these beings were not the same. These beings looked like human-sized bugs and were able to pop in and out of my reality. I was able to see them, their color a bright green, even in a waking state. They had large round mirror-like eyes that almost seemed to send a signal, making me feel certain emotions as if my emotions were being programmed for something later.

I learned to communicate with them later after undergoing some experimentation that was done on me with what I call "death perception." I was put under anesthesia once when I had my tonsils out but something happened. Something was different about the place and the people under the masks. They didn't seem human to me. I believe I received an implant that day. These implants, I feel, are tracking devices for the earth governments and secret societies similar to those of the

Thule and Vril societies of Nazi Germany. I believe secret societies really work with secret governments.

Many contactees and abductees, such as me, can have traumatic experiences and are monitored for the better part of their lives. People have been abducted by the government for experimentation, ritual purposes, or cooperative projects with non-terrestrial officers. Many non-terrestrial beings really don't want much to do with anything military because it simply isn't an issue where they are from. What I think happens is that monitoring happens after an initial experience with ET/ED's that have nothing to do with the military or government.

I feel that contactees are monitored by some esoteric secret part of our government because they are interested in the ongoing communications with these beings. This might be communication with our higher selves or the ET/ED part of us. Part of the human experience for many people includes feelings and experiences that are labeled "paranormal" but are common to people with psi sensitivity. After an ET/ED experience, humans can become very sensitive to the stranger instances in our lives like strong Deja vu and other sensations. Some people experience lost time, like a blackout, or wandering through the grey matter after trauma.

These government entities I encountered confused me a great deal for a long time until one day I was told by the beings I was in contact with that the implants are tracking devices. The actual ET/EDs do not need tracking devices or the use of implants because they use telepathy to communicate with. After a while I was in regular contact with those beings I call my "space family" and so was educated over time about a great many things by them. This has been a feature of my life from when I was young up until the present day. That is important for people to know because my contactee experiences tie in with my current research, how I feel led to look into various topics, and to some of the conclusions I draw in this book about the para-dimensional space art that is in the picture section of the book.

UFO EXPERIENCE

Sometimes I pick up visual imagery mentally, my space family communicating. I was shown ships in telepathic visits, in waking dreams. These ships were like nothing described or any I have seen. The ships were of a black, hexagon shape, moving as though someone was just telling it to move with their mind... fluid, like a fish in water. These ships can attach to one another like magnets, to form a bigger craft and once they're connected they moved together across the night sky with few lights to simulate stars.

I saw one of these craft, a UFO sighting for me, in 2003. The craft floated down in front of my van when I was traveling down Highway 10 about ten miles out of Phoenix, Arizona headed toward the New Mexico border.

It moved from the left side of the road to just in front of me as I was driving, about 1 0 or 1 2 feet away at the height of just about the size of a semi-truck. I thought I was going to hit it. I felt like I knew it wanted me to see it very clearly because it stayed right in front of my moving van, tracking with the speed of the vehicle, flying with precision.

As I came up to a building by the road, the UFO proceeded to speed up to the building, float over and hover. I drove toward it, and looking at it through the passenger side window, I saw it as it twirled while something from the bottom telescopically came out and went back in. The white lights of the craft turned to multicolored lights displayed and then back to a solid white. It took off like a helicopter, banking in front of me again, completely silent and with ease, it took no more than a few seconds for it to join with the others off into the distant mountains. A gentleman named Mr. John Bowen was with me and can verify this story.

MY ONCE AND FUTURE ART

Shortly after I arrived in East Texas I formed the "Moon Anomaly Research Society" inspired by the work of Helena Bloomfield, Neville Thompson, Ross Curley, and Andrew D. Basiago. Andrew Basiago had started the Mars Anomaly Research Society with a Facebook group I regularly participated in. There was a bit of confusion on the names both of which shared the acronym

M.A.R.S. which was pointed out by Andrew one day. So I changed my moon-based group's name to the Lunar Anomaly Research Society or "L.A.R.S." or LARS instead. I really appreciate Andrew who has been a great example to me as a researcher, an inspirational comrade in the search for evidence of extraterrestrial life.

In the LARS group, myself and other researchers talk about research into the many photographs from the space agencies that show structures and other artifacts on the moon. It is believed by many people that our space agencies have not been forthcoming about any information except that our moon is a lifeless body, devoid of an atmosphere with the overt color being nothing but ashen gray. My own research was driven by the finds of many other features that suggested buildings, towers and other structures in the photographs and sharing those.

However, my own work turned into a dance with the strange when I began to see surrealistic shapes, thematic scenes from dreamscape. Some scenes are extremely psychosexual and odd, so extreme as to be almost from nightmarish scenario. One day, a LARS member named

Amy Evans showed me a particular image, Mars image number MOC: M1 1 00099 from the surface of Mars. Something happened to my brain when I saw this image...

I recalled this image from the slide show shown to me when I was 15 years old.

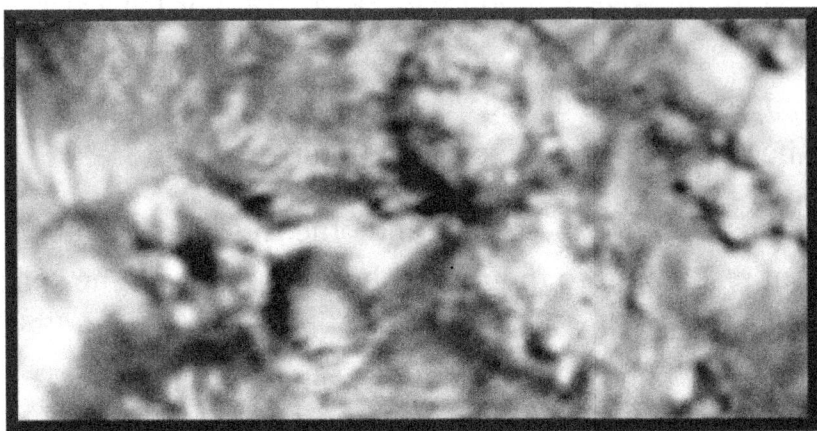

I began to research and find out that the image was not even supposed to have existed in 1982, the year I saw the slide show. This image was supposed to have been taken in 1997 and not released until the year 2000.

I found out later that Amy Evans is associated with Dr. Courtney Brown of the Farsight Institute and also is associated with Ken Johnson of NASA. Ken worked with an image department within that organization. This image is also the same image that Dr. Courtney Brown and his team remote-viewed and that can remote view session is documented on a video that can be seen online at http://www.farsight.org/demo/Mysteries/Mysteries_1/Mysteries_Project_1.html

As I looked deeper into the image as suggested by Amy, I saw the exact images I was shown in 1 982 and began to wonder why I was seeing them. It was deeply perplexing to me as I began to find many of those images I was shown in a dark classroom slide show many years ago. What could this mean? I went on the supposition for a long time that the space agencies were somehow inserting this strange imagery into their photographs. I could not figure out why.

I did know that whenever people found such imagery, the meme appeal to the concept of "pareidolia" was cited. Pariedolia is a trick of human perception where a person sees shapes in random input, such as animals in clouds going by in the sky.

Pariedolia is often utilized by pseudo skeptics to supposedly debunk the visualization work of anomalists. This tactic is not very effective within the research community of anomalists and is generally disregarded, unless the debunker also has a plausible theory besides, the "It's just a rock" theory. We call those kinds of debunkers, "Rockists."

At first, I thought the surreal images were placed there as some kind of "intentional pariedolia"... to have people find weird stuff and either be repulsed or confused by it, or to seed the debunking process with false data. Then I thought, due to the graphic nature of some of the imagery, that the surreal imagery was put there as some kind of subliminal experiment to either ferret out individuals who could see them for some reason or to psychologically repulse people unconsciously so that they would stop looking at the images and go find something better to do with their time.

I was stuck with the fact that they showed them specifically to me and one other student back in 1 982 and that was the twist of strange I just could not figure out to be congruent with the "intentional pariedolia" or "subliminal" theories. Why would they ask a 15-year-old boy from the past about these particular images? Also, as I amassed a larger and larger collection of such imagery, I realized that integration of the subject matter into the images was far too complex. The space agencies, NASA or whoever, couldn't have embedded the surrealistic content in their images.

I was kind of at a mysterious dead end, theory-wise.

One day Karen Christine Patrick, member of LARS and also the administrator of the Earth Anomaly Research Society, made an important breakthrough suggestion. It was an astonishing idea that broke open my understanding and explained my personal history with all of this.

Karen and I had both been part of the Mars Anomaly Research Society group of Andrew Basiago, but the friend we both now call "Andy" is also known for another group, Project Pegasus. Andy was a participant as a child in a program called

Project Pegasus where he and other children were sent through time to different events and brought back. Andy, when he was a kid, was shown a document which was his "Life on Mars" paper that he was to later write as an adult. Karen suggested that maybe I had been subject to such a time travel program, only in this case, my work was the very images I was discovering now, made into a slide show and brought back to be shown to my 1 5-year-old self in 1982.

This tied the whole thing together for me. This is an astonishing realization because I realize that what I am seeing is of such importance, for some reason I still cannot guess for sure, that a government "Op", or operation was created to either trigger me to see this, or to ask my teenager self what the heck this all means. The slide show images are in the very book you are reading, therefore, this might be the very images utilized in the slideshow, so please make note of the fact that you might be reading a book where the images may have been brought back to the past. This is, quite possibly, a time-traveling book.

I could not possibly include all the images that I have done where I have found surrealistic imagery. I have much more than what is included in this book. I tried to stick to the ones I remember seeing so long ago. The sheer volume as well as my contactee experiences has convinced me that I am seeing embedded extra-dimensional or extra-terrestrial communication of some kind. Other people are now being able to see this as well within the LARS group.

In this particular time, we are on the threshold of humanity discovering, for sure, that we are not alone in the Universe and never have been. The attempt is being made to shout this out loudly and in evidence format to humanity since, pretty much, the governments of the world had plenty of time to reveal what they know, but are not motivated to do this. It's the people, experiencers most specifically, that are going to pave the way for that disclosure.

This has been my path, to find these whimsical images embedded in official space agency photographs, illustrate them as evidence of ET/ED intelligence, and to share them. The only way I have found to display these images so that people can see them, is through art interpretation of these space images.

Bret Colin Sheppard ~ Bio

Team Sheppard and Patrick is the research team of Bret Colin Sheppard and Karen Christine Patrick.

Bret Colin Sheppard experienced a time anomaly where his anomaly finds from the future were shown to him in art class at his high school, where he was told that it was "art from various artists." Whoever did this time mission also knew that Bret has a photographic memory and this would be locked into his memory until a later time?

Years later, he feels compelled to pursue looking for anomalies in space agency images of the moon and Mars. He started a Facebook group for anomalists to share their finds called the Lunar Anomaly Research Society. He is known in the anomaly community for some of his discoveries, the Lunar Acropolis, the "Jupiter 2 UFO on Mars" and the Lion of Cydonia. Bret is writing his book on his anomaly finds, plus what he found deconstructing the manipulation of photos from our space agencies. His forthcoming book is called "Digital Moon"

THE BLUE BEINGS
Reverand John M. Polk

Saturday, August 29, 2015: At approximately 8:00 pm that evening, the visitors arrived. I can only speculate how they arrived, but perhaps it was like on Star Trek when Captain Kirk would be saying, "Beam us down, Scotty." I imagine that four individuals teleport and materialize right in front of the double doors to a conference room. What happens next is not my imagination, but what I saw, plus what others said they saw as well.

Jennifer Stein had just wrapped up her introduction to Travis Walton's new documentary entitled, "Travis." Immediately after, a curious crew of four individuals came through the door and approached me with cash-in-hand, asking if I'm the one they pay to watch Travis. I quickly found Debbie Hewins, who located her twin sister, Audrey "Starborn" Hewins, the founder of Starborn Support International and the organizer of Experiencers Speak 4, who ultimately collected their money. They then sat down, maybe 20 feet, in front of me.

Later on, Audrey told me that it seemed they had no concept of paper currency and didn't realize how much they even had. They didn't even have enough money to cover all four of them for the event, but Audrey let them come in anyway. It seemed odd to her the way the leader of the group offered her the money. With both palms open, his hands side-by-side, the paper currency was simply laying in his hands. Audrey looked at him and could tell that he didn't understand our primitive monetary system. Audrey said to give her four of "those," I'm assuming twenties, and then she let them in. At the time, I didn't think anything of it.

Not too long into the Travis documentary, the youngest one got up and walked around around one of the eight-person, round tables and then sat back down. He must have repeated this behavior 6 or 7 times in the exact same fashion. At the conclusion of the documentary, Travis conducted a Q and A for maybe a half an hour. Immediately following, the group of four approached me and the oldest one wanted to talk. At this juncture, I'm going to give a short description of each.

"DON"

The being I had the most interaction with, observed the most, and his appearance is burned into my memory. Don is the oldest being. He seemed "grandfatherly." He identified himself as "Don." He seemed to be about 60-65 years old in appearance. He was probably my height and weight, 5'9" and 165 lbs. He wore white sneakers, blue jeans, a nondescript flannel shirt, and a hat similar to a ball cap but more like a fishing hat, beige in color. He pulled it curiously low over his face, glasses, and eyes. In the breast pocket of his flannel shirt, he had what appeared to be sunglasses. He had the most prominently blue shade of skin of the group, and unusually large ears.

"SONNY"

The next visitor I call, "Sonny." I thought maybe he was Don's son. He looked to be in his mid-thirties, was tall and thin, with blondish hair, parted on the side. These two visitors had grayish-blue skin. The grandfather had more of a blue complexion than his son.

"KIDD"

There was another being, I thought to be Don's grandson, I nicknamed him "Kidd." He was about 6'1" and wearing a hoodie, shorts, and sneakers. He was average weight. He had dark-brown to black hair, a fair-to-mild olive complexion, and black eyes void of any color..... just two big, black empty spheres in his eye orbits. To me, he kind of looked like Jason Martell, from the show "Ancient Aliens" who is an accomplished researcher. The grandson came up to me, standing in front of my vendor table, with Don and the others to my left, beside my table and in front of the conference room double-door main entrance.

At one point, the grandson then looked me in the eyes, ready to speak with me and said, "The Anunnaki, the Anunnaki, the Anunnaki, the Anunnaki...," over and over about 5 or 6 times. Almost like a child that has autism, his behavior was that of someone who is mentally challenged.

Ironically, in Travis Walton's or Grant Cameron's presentation, I can't recall which one, there was a clip from the movie, "Rainman" where Dustin Hoffman saw a box of 250 toothpicks that fell on the ground and he started saying, "246, 246 yeah 246." Tom Cruise said that the box says 250. Rainman kept saying, "246, 246, 246" and he was correct.

But the showing of the movie clip occurred before the four visitors arrived at the conference, so he couldn't have been imitating the behavior. I then took a deep, penetrating look at him and was astonished to realize that his eyes were completely black. They were absent of color and lifeless, without emotion, like he was biologically created and not born with a soul.

This to me is reminiscent of the "Star Children" that have been seen all over the world as well as the "black-eyed children" that people have encountered. They are often almost robotic in their speech and movements and can only recite a few short sentences over and over again.

Ron Scharfy, one of the witnesses to the visitors, postulates that the grandson saying, "The Anunnaki" over and over again could have acted as a trigger mechanism to place me in an altered state of consciousness with memory gaps.

My belief is that his hypothesis, may in fact, be true. Right around that time, I started to have "missing time" and to forget what I was doing. I refer to this syndrome as ET administering, "Alien Anesthesia," a phenomenon that has been reported by many abductees and experiencers. "MARK" The fourth visitor, I was calling him the "Martian Dude" but now that I'm giving them all names, I am calling him "Mark." He was 5 ft. tall, and at the most, maybe 130 lbs. with a bald, white head, pale white skin, small tight-fitting sunglasses and a goatee beard extending maybe 4 or 5 inches straight down from the bottom of his chin. He had no facial hair except for the black beard. I can't exactly remember his shoes, but I think they were moccasins. He had on blue jeans and a white sleeveless t-shirt, the effect of it all resembling a biker in appearance.

"JANE"

Some of the other witnesses, Audrey Hewins, Keith Andrews and others, out of the over-20 witnesses to the event, witnessed a large, blonde woman wearing a sweater, who was apparently with the visitors. At no time did I see this person and I am a key witness to this whole event, so I haven't figured out why my observations are different from others, yet. However, I do believe she was present. I just never noticed her myself. Maybe I wasn't supposed to perceive her.

From what I gather from Audrey and other witnesses, she

accompanied them as they first entered the conference room. I did not see a woman. It was strange, because I saw four beings and most people said four. Many saw a woman and I have been calling her, "Jane" for reference. She, too, had blue skin and spoke with a Spanish or Mexican accent, according to Audrey. I am including other people's accounts for this because I am not a direct witness to a woman in the group. The following story was told on the "Stary Time" podcast with Bran and Dave (starytimepodcast@gmail.com).

They had heard from Audrey "Starborn" Hewins what was said about the woman in the group. Audrey said the term "blonde" to them, the Blue Beings, referring to a woman that was with them. They reacted as if they did not know what "blonde" meant. Audrey saw a big, blonde woman with them. Since we know that ET can shape-shift or can alter the perception of us humans, it's possible that different people were seeing a different configuration of aliens in the group.

VISTING WITH THE VISITORS

As soon as Travis Walton wrapped up his Q & A, the four visitors got out of their chairs and approached me. Don began a dialogue with me. He was standing very close, "in my personal space" for some reason, within inches of me almost the whole time.

After the fact, I spoke with Audrey Hewins of this visitor and she said he told her his name was "Don." Don initiated the conversation with me first by saying that his son, who looked more like his grandson by age appearance, had been drugged by his step-father and was now in his custody. I replied by saying that I was happy for him and his son, that now he was with his real father, and that he could take care of him and nurse him back to health.

Don then asked about my book, "YAHWEH, The Biblical God, Is An Alien." I then explained it to him briefly, showing him a print copy, seeing if he wanted to buy a copy of the book. I also showed him on my Mac that the book was available as an ebook on my website (JohnPolkMedia.com). His interest was lost shortly after that, as if God in the Earth Bible being an alien was old news across the Milky Way.

I then did a demonstration of my pendulums and allowed the spirit force that pulses through me to spin them both at different rates simultaneously. (http://tinyurl.com/pendulumfiremagic)

This captured his interest briefly, then people were starting to surround us and it seemed Don welcomed the attention. Then intense interest became an impromptu interview as conference attendees were spinning questions at Don.

As I said before, my focus was soon redirected to the grandson, "Kidd" who came up to me standing in front of my table as Don was "holding court" with the small, gathering crowd right there. That was exactly when the grandson then looked me in the eyes, and said, "The Anunnaki, the Anunnaki, the Anunnaki, the Anunnaki," over and over. Exactly then, I forgot what I was doing.

ALIEN ANESTHESIA

What I experienced at that moment, I refer to as an ET administering "Alien Anesthesia" ... some energy or hypnotic thought projection that makes people in those situations start to have missing time and forget or have a foggy recollection. It is a frequent aspect of alien encounters, as many experiencers will attest. Once you are placed under Alien Anesthesia, you remember only what the ETs want you to remember, if you can remember anything at all.

One thing you can try, is to get a seasoned professional with years of experience with Experiencers to perform a hypnotic regression. Many experiencers have gone that route to recall what happened to them. You can get some help finding an "experiencer friendly" professional hypnotist through the F.R.E.E organization mentioned before, at Experiencer.org

Alternatively, one can always entertain the possibility that you can slowly, "Pop your alien memory cap." This is another phrase I have coined. I encourage people to be patient as well, and not to expect the whole recall to come back, to all at once. First it will come to you like short movie scenes or video clips. Eventually, it may come back to you as a full 3-5 minute "movie trailer." Educating yourself on other experiencer cases also helps.

"YOUR SKIN IS BLUE"

When I then returned my attentions back to Don, I noticed a crowd was now formed around us, and he looked comfortable and loose while talking and fielding questions. At this juncture, the Jedi Mind Trick they had laid on me is settling in deep.

My eyes deeply fixated on Don's eyes, face, and skin color. I noticed that even his fingernails were gray. At this juncture, I was posturing mentally to say out loud, in front of everyone, "Your skin is blue." Keith Andrews, another witness to the ETs, beat me to it, though I couldn't remember that it was him at the time.

Later, after speaking with Keith Andrews, he told me it was he that had said it and Don went on to say, "I am a shifter and a healer." Now Don was commanding everyone's attention. Keith then asked him if he was Pleiadian and Don responded, "Yes."

Keith then mentioned that he had come in contact with a Martokian (Martian) in the past. That seemed to pique Don's interest. Don replied by saying something to the effect, "Where and when did you see a Martokian, and why was one here (meaning on Earth)?" Keith then asked Don if he could take a picture of him and Don responded, "Yes," but followed up by saying that he could not share it with anyone. Keith respectfully agreed.

Keith did show some people the photo at Audrey Hewins retreat at her parent's house after the conference, but he will not share the picture online. Some people think that this is all a tall-tale regarding the picture, however, I believe Keith because multiple people saw it including Audrey, Lynn Hartrum, Grant Cameron and Dave Scott, host of "Spaced Out Radio." Dave, a brilliant host by the way, lives close to Keith in British Columbia, Canada. Dave did not attend the conference or the retreat, but did see the picture in Keith's phone.

While Keith was speaking with Don, in the back of my mind, I was thinking to ask Don his name because, at that point, I had not yet found out his name until days later when I learned it from Audrey. I decided to try and take a picture and then follow them into the parking lot just to see where would they go. How they had arrived? In a car? In a spacecraft?

Mysteriously, I forgot to do all of the above. I was in some kind of awake state of paralysis. This also happened to Ron Scharfy, at least as far as trying to take a picture of the beings departing.

Ron had been taking multiple photos and videos during most of the conference. Shortly thereafter, the other tall, thin, human-looking, blue-skinned ET "Sonny" could tell that Don was feeling far too comfortable. He then said in his ear at least 2 or 3 times, "We have to go, we have to go." Right after the four (or possibly five) of them had departed, Keith Andrews said, "We just witnessed Pleiadians."

Minutes later, Ron Scharfy went outside to take a phone call and saw a pulse of white light illuminate the sky over the hotel for a split second, and then vanish. Ron interpreted this flash of light as a ship, space-time vehicle or vortex, opening and closing. It seems this same pulse of white light was seen at Audrey's retreat at her parent's house following the conference. It was reported by witnesses to the after-conference social time that many paranormal things happened.

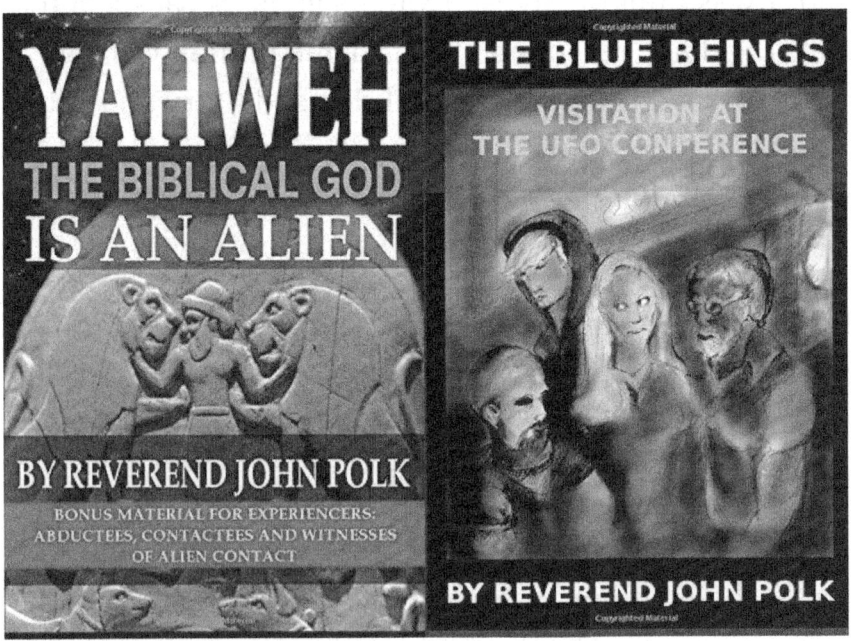

Reverend John M. Polk ~ Bio

The Reverend John Marcus Polk is an International Metaphysical Minister, a Reiki Master Teacher, and a medium. Reverend Polk was born in 1969 in Raleigh, North Carolina. He holds a Bachelor of Arts degree in Broadcasting, and another Bachelor of Arts Degree in Metaphysics from the University of Sedona. This university granted John the title of International Metaphysical Minister after his studies were completed. John is also a Reiki Master, and an instructor in Usui Reiki.

He is the founder of Wolf Spirit Ministries, LLC. In addition to all of this, John was gifted with the ability to be a Channel and a medium. In his book "Yahweh, the Biblical God, is an Alien" John adds his insights into Ancient Alien theory as a theologian, in the area of exo-spirituality. Reverend Polk is a psychic medium, making contact with the ancestral spirit, aliens, and ghosts. He lives in Florida and works on writing and media projects sharing messages globally.

I'M AN EXPERIENCER

Growing up in a three story condo on the ocean in Daytona Beach set the stage for a lifetime of abductions for me to come. One night when I was 15 years old, I was lying in bed while listening to the crashing waves that served as a kind of soothing lullaby. Next thing I knew, I opened my eyes to see three greys looking in through my sliding glass door. Like little kids, they were pressing their heads against the glass and before I knew what happened, they were in my room without opening the door. Then, a light captured my attention as it bounced off the rolling waves. Exceedingly bright was this light cascading into my bedroom, however it was not blinding to gaze upon.

Just then, I blacked out and awoke the next day thinking it was all a dream. Later that day, I began experiencing discomfort in my private areas and soon arrived at the conclusion that I had undergone a procedure or operation. A few days removed, the pain subsided and I went about life as if nothing extraordinary had occurred. Shortly thereafter, I began writing a book of poetry entitled, "Beyond Oblivion, Through The Crevices In Between."

Back in 1985, I wrote off the encounter as if it was a dream but then in 2009, I started to relive it and other encounters through flashback visions, just like quick clips from a movie montage. Eventually, I came to the sobering realization that I had been abducted numerous times and it took me until age 40 to pop my alien memory cap and remember. From then on, my blind folded past started to bleed through into my conscious mind and I started seeing ET's and UFO's unlike ever before.

As I am a medium, I began questioning my guides and digging deep into my subconscious in search of extraterrestrial answers. What I found exceeded all my supernatural expectations. The aliens chose me to see them and their spacecrafts for the rest of my life.

I am an experiencer and abductee who communicates with the other side. Navigating the Astral Plane since I was a teenager has always been exciting and adventurous for me. The one thing I failed to realize is that not only am I in contact with spiritual entities, but I'm also channeling extraterrestrials telepathically. Enoch, the scribe of the gods, and Yahweh or Enlil of the Anunnaki, masquerading as God in the Bible and are the two that send me the most information.

Now, facing my greatest fears, I'm coming out of the closet to let Experiencers from all around the world know that you are not alone. The best thing for all of us is to share our encounters with others because as the word spreads, more experiencers will speak out as the fear ridicule will rapidly diminish. Plus, the spoken word manifests an abundance of energies that enables the Earth and we Earthlings to ascend closer to the light and enlightenment. So now, let us all join hands together within the collective God consciousness that we are all a part of and reach out to foundations like Dr. Edgar Mitchell's FREE, The Foundation For Research Into Extraterrestrial Encounters who are here to help us.

Reverend John Marcus Polk

Born: July 30, 1969

Raleigh, North Carolina

407-924-8857

jpolk2@cfl.rr.com

www.johnpolkmedia.com

www.alienoraclescrolls.com

Education And Credentials:

*Ancient Alien Astronaut Theorist – Bible Aliens.

* Author, "Yahweh, The Biblical God, Is An Alien" Available on gumroad.com E Book and createspace.com, a division of Amazon, in paperback. Go to johnpolkmedia.com for more info.

1) Articles: Dr. Rudy Schild, Astrophysicist Harvard Smithsonian, Quantum Hologram Theory.

* "Quantum Hologram Matrix" podcast. Host and

Executive Producer. Airs live every Wednesday 8-10 pm EST on beyondthestrange.com.

* Aquarianradio.com Cohost every Friday 8-10 pm EST. Numerous shows archived.

1) Plus, countless guest appearances on other shows and networks.

* Opening Speaker Experiencers Speak 4 & Starborn Support International, UFO Conference 08/28/15.

* "Ancient Aliens, Anunnaki And The Gods," Webinar paid panel member 06/18/16.

* International Metaphysical Minister, University of Sedona.

* B. A. Metaphysics, University of Sedona.

* Reiki Master/Teacher Usui Reiki.

* B. A. Broadcasting, Concord College, Athens, WV.

* Founder, Wolf Spirit Ministries, LLC.

* Consultant for Dr. Edgar Mitchell's FREE, The Foundation For Research Into Extraterrestrial Encounters, Experiencer.org

TIME TO BE HUMAN
Janet Kira Lessin

Somewhere between the ages of one and two while I spent most of my days still in the crib thinking not of time, age or space, I received a farewell visitation from my galactic family. Puzzled I stood and watched while hundreds of beings appeared all around me, all different species, no two alike. These beings positioned themselves one after another rotating to the front of the line where our eyes met to say goodbye to me.

Fascinated, I looked around my bedroom and saw beings encircled me 360 degrees. Their sacred ritual resembled a snake dance and stretched through the cosmos beyond my view. They took turns and rotated to the front of the line to appear directly before me. Each took great took care to make eye contact, send energy and share breath with me, one after another.

I saw their souls through the right eye where the singularity exists, a window through the cosmos all the way home to Source where I reunited with Source, the unity state of consciousness from where all life originated. I saw the cosmos, sped through time and space to Source where I felt love emanate from them. With friendly faces, eyes beamed love, each attempted to smile. Sometimes they were unable either because they lacked a mouth or lacked the ability to smile. They waited their turn to send me loving energy from their hearts. And if they lacked a heart, love beamed from them. I felt joy emanate from each being.

I stood frozen, watching them, fixated on this dance, tiny hands held tightly to my crib bars so I wouldn't fall. Time flew by, endless, timeless. Highly energized after receiving all that good will, I smiled, laughed, giggled and greeted each in turn. Some were familiar, all were friendly and welcome. I felt elated, such extreme joy and bliss. The height of my life thus far and the best part of my eternal existence, our reunion completed my soul.

The last being greeted me. In a moment of time that stretched through eternity, the procession ended, the rotation ceased and all became quiet, silence complete. With reverence and love, respect and appreciation, the moment to part came at last. It seemed all took a deep breath and held it. When they exhaled, with a clap so loud it sounded like thunder, the portal closed.

The ritual done, I disconnected from them and fell deep within my body till at last, fully embodied, I locked into my human self for the duration of this journey. Now I was forever limited, like all mortals and could no longer zoom around the galaxies. I could, however, travel using my astral body. But never again would I travel in such an extensive and conscious way like before.

At that point I could no longer speak with intelligence. Even my thoughts were jumbled, confused and incomplete. I struggled to focus, to remember and recall. Where is my memory? What happened and why? Frustrated I cried out. My words were unintelligible. Gone were my language skills. My intellect now fragmented and incomplete, I could only speak baby talk from that moment on. Like the Biblical Tower of Babel, I could only babble.

Infuriated, I screamed till a deep roar let loose from deep within my soul. The pain of such complete and final separation from my eternal family and God-Source itself threatened to shred my soul. Anguished, nothing emerged from my vocal chords but gibberish and baby talk. Tears swelled from my eyes, ran down my checks. I bawled till my mother sound asleep down the hall from the bedroom at the rear of the house, woke with a start and rushed to my side. Mother thought I needed rescued. Genuinely afraid for me, she picked me up and examined me, certain that a noise that loud could only come from someone severely injured.

I cried loudly "Mommy, mommy, I saw monsters in my room."

"No, no!" my mind screamed. "That's not what I mean! Why did my mouth and tongue betray me, replaced the word friends with the word monster? How can that be? What kind of trick is this?"

Uninjured but merely frightened by invisible monsters under my bed, Mom felt comforted.

Once again I tried to explain and again, that same monster gibberish came from my mouth.

"What?" I thought as I heard my mouth jumble the words I formed in my head. "No, no! Not monsters but hundreds of kind, loving beings visited my room. Why can't she understand me?

Mom tried to console me. Inconsolable, I cried even harder.

I cried, "Mommy, mommy, monsters! Monsters!"

Again I spoke clearly the words generated in my mind. Perplexed, unable to understand how did incorrect words continued to emanate from my mouth? After this, the third and final attempt I felt hopeless and totally frustrated. With nothing left to do, I sobbed uncontrollably. I just let it go, the floodtides of tears rushed forth till exhausted, I could cry no more. I whimpered as my mother kissed my forehead, wiped my tears and laid me down.

I cried so hard for so long, my nose plugged. Mom retrieved a tissue and bringing it to my tiny nose, encouraged me to blow. Making sure I could breathe, she left.

Wiping tears from my red, now swollen eyes, mother tucked me in, kissed me and left. Mortal bound and just a baby, I reluctantly began to resign myself to my fate. I thought as she left that I didn't want to live here. I wanted to go "home" and my soul knew just where to find it. Too bad I could breathe. If I couldn't then perhaps I could return there?

I cried myself silly and begged for sleep. My head spinning with exhaustion, my now invisible friends granted my wish and mercifully sleep overwhelmed me. As I drifted off, gentle thoughts caressed my mind. "Sleep, little one, sleep. It's time to forget."

"Remember we're always with you and will never leave you. In time you'll awaken. But until then, you must sleep the deep sleep of life and travel great distances down the river of dreams. Many adventures await you. You will suffer great pain to know intense joy. All the while, you'll forget till the right time comes. And when that time arrives, we will tell you, "It's time."

Next morning memories of my existence before this life began to fade from the foreground. I struggled to remember. I allowed a level of forgetting in order to be about my mission and do what I must. With new found clarity I knew that in order to succeed, the mission I chose when I came here must be first and foremost.

But a part of me vowed never to forget. Someday I will no longer be able to contain myself, stifle my words and memories will rush back and dominate my consciousness. Shamed, ridiculed and hurt, tides change and the planetary paradigm shift begins. More accept experiencer testimonials than ever, create the energy for those like me to come forth and share our versions of reality. Ultimately each must choose what to believe personally. If you're here, drawn to read this book and witness these accounts, odds are you too may have experienced strange things. Whether you believe or not, I do appreciate you reading this. If something resonates, fine. If not, so be it, so it is.

If so, then please take it to the next step and give it to higher parts of yourself to judge and evaluate. Soon we remember who our true soul nature, necessary in order to save this world from destruction. We now awaken and take responsibility for our own unconscious acts and attitudes. We demand transparency from those who don't love us and desire to control us or wish us dead. We stand firm in integrity and affirm our connection to it all. We remember for the time has come to awaken.

ALIEN ENCOUNTERS
Korey Lavoie

When I went to Nevada a few years ago to stay with family for a year, the cosmic energies of the American West activated repressed memories of critical incidences from my formative years. While there I had strange encounters with owls, a rabbit under the Moon, a blue-white light with a smaller red-light above it and intense dreams that marked the passage of time.

As I look back at these various incidences I recognize some of these events created memory markers. Our subconscious mind marks the location of repressed and forgotten memories of intense, emotional encounters, such as paranormal events and alien contact until its safe for the conscious mind to recall. These markers often house keys to major events.

After I returned from Nevada my mind kept circling back to a time when I wrote a short story in grade school when I was 7 years old. In the story I wrote that the power went out late one winter night when my mother and I arrived home. Aliens came into the house but I was able to chase them off with a flash-light.

I wondered why I had written that story. But suddenly, like a fish breaking the water's surface, I realized, "Oh, that story's based on something that actually happened!" My mind responded to a visual snap shot of what had been curtained off, probably for my safety. An image of someone in the house that night acted as a catalyst for my mind to shift, remember and integrate a memory that had been closed off in a darkened portion of my mind.

I remembered my parents were separated at that time and because my mother worked a late shift, I spent nights with my bloodline father. I woke up one winter's evening and my mother and father were engaged in a weird conversation. Mom spoke in a slow, deliberate and disconnected tone of voice. She said was here to pick me up and take me home. My father thought her behavior was so odd and out of the ordinary, he asked her if she was drunk.

"No, I'm here to pick Korey up. Come on Korey Honey! Get dressed. Let's go!" Dad protested asked her what was going on. Mom just reiterated that she was here to get me. I, curious, knew something odd was happening. But I felt strangely nonchalant as I put on my snow-suit. In my hand I held a play-school flash-light. Mom was silent all the way home and strangely, I didn't ask her why she came to pick me up. But I do remember that the dash-board clock in the car displayed 11 o' clock.

As we neared the house, I noticed a bright-blue light emanating from a source that looked like a bright metallic disk hanging over the neighbor's front yard directly across the street. It lit up the entire yard. As we got out of the car and walked up the steps to the house, I asked Mom where the light came from. She said: "It's the neighbors honey, don't look." For some reason, I listened.

We walked into the house, closed the door behind us and

I went and stood in the middle of the front-room of the double-wide we lived in. Mom headed straight for the kitchen and tried the lights. "The power's out," She said as she flicked the light and nothing happened. I wondered what produced the blue light that filled the house so brightly since the power in the house was out and there were no street-lights in my neighborhood.

Our home, a double-wide trailer with a sheet-metal-facade and metal door had a rubber-seal that made a distinct sound whenever it was opened or closed. Despite the fact that the door was shut and that it didn't open, movement at the door caught my eye.

I saw a figure standing there and because of its height, I actually thought: "What is another kid doing here?" then, I noticed the bulbous, pale-grey colored head, the form-fitting black-jumpsuit and spindly build. The moment I realized I thought: "It's not another kid," I wondered, "What is it?" The entity rushed at me moving like an insect. It seemed to have perfect muscle balance and control which enabled it to move in a swift and fluid motion.

I stood at least six feet away from him. Despite the distance he was in front of me in an instant. I can't even clearly remember the moment I met his gaze, it was as though the moment he stopped in front of me, I was thrust into a black-void, yet with an impression of pink-light or mist surrounding me with a feeling as though my body were hit with a neurological shock. Maybe I was seeing light through my own eyelids or blood vessels at the moment of induction. The next thing that occurred in my conscious memory at that time was that I was standing in the living room with awareness of my body and where I was, only the Blue-light was gone and I couldn't see a thing. Because it seemed as though only an instant had passed, I thought that the light had just shut off and that the entity was still standing right in front of me. So I switched on the flash-light in my hand and shone it in front of me, only to reveal that both my Mother and I had moved so that we were facing each other and were now standing near the Kitchen.

She asked me what I was doing up. I asked her if she had seen anyone else in the house. She paused briefly and said: "You had a bad-dream Korey, go back to bed." I turned and walked away towards me room, noting on some level that we were both still dressed in our winter-clothes. I felt too tired and strange to really think about what had happened, yet after I stripped out of my snow-suit and lay down in bed, I noticed that dawn was just starting to break through the window outside.

So, that was the memory that opened up my recall and more followed, which I will share with you all as I update and write this out. If you know how a Marker works, It's like a catalyst that reacts with other common memories hidden within your mind. Once you find one thread, it exerts a pull and shines light upon further experiences. Not only did other visitations start to come back to me but details of that evening came out as well. I've never undergone regression for my experiences so details are vague and I don't have substantial memories of events on-board ships.

I describe the ability that these entities have to over-rule our conscious mind in terms of how Rupert Sheldrake explored and conducted experiments with the capacity of People to tell when they are being stared at by another person. If you were to scale that ability up appropriately for how advanced intelligences would be able to utilize it, you could induce a powerful hypnotic state in beings lacking a comparably evolved capacity -not that we have no such capacities- with the same kind of ease and proficiency that myself and others recall.

However, something important occurred to me: Why was it that I could remember when they would show up and this in-between state where I was about to be bought on board a craft but little else? I realized that it must have to do with the "Tractor-beam" technology that they use to bring people on board in the first place. This Blue-white light focused on me as I stood in the living room surrounded by these entities and I could feel it synching with my body, the sensation reminded me of floating on a stream, only diffused throughout my body in terms of the pull of current.

Passing through the window-glass is a common experience and as I recall, Dr. David Jacobs pointing out, it is commonly reported that these entities show a preference for taking us through windows and serves as further confirmation that we are not concocting fantasies or other-wise delusional. As improbable as it seems that a physical body could be moved through glass without breaking it: The fact that there is a technical limitation to this ability implicit in their having a more difficult time phasing people through walls and a preference for using windows is telling. A figment of imagination wouldn't be confined as such.

Passing through the glass was like a change in pressure. I'd liken it to diving in slow-motion but what I've come to realize is that this technology must synch with and effectively phase-lock with the body's bio-photo-electric resonant field. In my case, I can only conclude that the reason why it is necessary for those being taken aboard in this way to be in a semi-conscious state is because the pull this phase-lock exerts on atomic structure would cause the physical body to disintegrate if we were affected by it in without having a degree of conscious awareness of the body to hold itself together.

Another aspect of this experience that is compelling is that years later, I was sitting looking out through that same window and I just had a sense that it was significant somehow. Eventually, that house was torn down and I had intended to take a piece of glass from that pane, unfortunately, I didn't get the chance.

As far as other significant encounters from my Childhood, I guess the next would be an implantation incident, of which I have two that I recall clearly. Probably the most drastic of these had a flash of extreme pain associated with it as a marker; it began on a midsummer's day in the house when I was around 8 or 9 if I'm remembering right. Just Mom and I at the house that day, you know how you can sense when someone is in the house with you in another room? All of a sudden, I lost the sense that she was anywhere in the house and things just got really quiet, I was thinking of looking for her but I had the impulse to go lay down in my room instead. At the time, I was staying in a kind of spare-room off the hall with a simple curtain over the entry-way for privacy.

I went in and lay down on my right side facing the wall but I heard movement in the hallway and turned my head over my shoulder to look, I saw the curtain part and there are two things interesting about that. First of all, if it had been my Mother or any person of average height, I should have been able to see them from the angle I was looking at. Whoever came into my room was short. The other thing is, it's like they can use a kind of Jedi-mind trick, I had the sudden impulse to close my eyes and look away and that is exactly what I did. It's like they can reach inside your consciousness to find the impulse that they want you to obey and insert that as an imperative action.

I heard someone approach my bed and pause, at the moment of formulating my conscious response of trying to figure out who was there: I felt this agonizing pain in my back so intense that I blacked out; the pain was gigantic and overwhelming. When I came back, I was looking down into the crevice between the wall and my mattress and I heard a voice in my head that sounded eerily like my Grandfather's say: "You can roll over now." I did so and saw what I can only vaguely remember as three beings wearing white in my room with me. The voice then said: "What we have just given you will aid you when this occurs."

I wrote a poem where I included a line about the vision

that was then projected in front of my Minds-eye and described it thus: "I see a vision of Gaia wreathed in flames but she does not burn." It was as though the Earth were kindled with and throwing off this massive, Golden-white-greenish energy that seemed to flicker like a fire. I think that they just left the room after that and I just kind of lay there zoned out and flummoxed for a while before just trying to go on with my day.

Later on, however, Mom was going over my bed and called out to me, "Korey! Your shirt is ripped!" She noticed a small puddle on the sheet right where my lower back would have been: "There's blood here! What happened?" I couldn't tell her what had happened, either the memory was already sinking into the abyss of my subconscious or I just didn't want to talk about it but I did tell her the truth: "I don't know." I have no idea where that shirt is now. Another relic lost, oh well.

There's something significant in how they used my Grandfather's voice to telepathically communicate with me. There was an incident where I was holding a Styrofoam glider in his house and he asked me to give it back to him in a demanding tone, something may have gotten mixed up between his request and orders I'd received on board ship from entities that had ordered me around at some point. Because I flat out panicked and ran off, accidently breaking the plane in the process. Everyone was stunned and knew that something had happened; even he was more concerned than angry because he saw the look in my eyes before I broke and ran.

Anyway, the other implantation experience occurred in the same curtained off room one evening as I was trying to sleep, it all happened very fast. A short "Grey" with dark tannish brown skin wearing a red shirt rushed into the room, grabbed my head with one hand and slammed a probe up through my right nostril in through my Sinus-cavity and in towards my Brain. Then he left just as quickly. Cue long-term problems with Nose-bleeds that have mercifully cleared up since then, what happened next at least helped me confirm that something out of the ordinary happened and also served as a marker for that event. Yet I still feel betrayed by my Mother for it.

I didn't even call out for her, I just lay there dazed but she came down the hall calling my name. So she knew something was up, I still didn't respond, just lay there as she came over and looked at me . . . Something that strikes me as even more odd now that I think about it, because I'm not sure if I just wanted to pretend that it hadn't happened or didn't want her to know what had happened. She asked me in this disconcerted tone: "Your nose is bleeding, why your nose is bleeding?" I told the truth, that someone had come into the room and stuck something up my nose. She got really quiet and then her entire demeanor changed as she hissed at me: "You picked it!" I tried to protest but she just got more adamant and enraged: "You lay there and you picked it!" Her tone brokered no argument and she simply turned and left the room.

That pretty much sums up the response that my experiences and trying to tell them why I was so frightened at night garnered from my family. They didn't want to deal with what was going on, or be in anyway supportive of me in my distress because it would have entailed facing and admitting that something strange was happening. Worse yet, being at the obvious nexus of craft dropping by the house and strange people scampering around, I feel like I must have been a harbinger for the family I was born into this didn't help with feelings they expressed towards me and acted out on in some awful ways.

In another instance, I was at my grandparent's house one day, once again, an eerie silence descended over the house. I was compelled to hide-out behind a pair of chairs in the living room. I heard something coming towards me and at first; I thought it must have been the cat coming to visit me. Then, I saw the hand of an entity with dark-tan skin and three long fingers reach into view and grasped the runner of the chair. He crawled near and stuck his head into my hiding-spot, turned and looked at me.

I had an impression of him thinking "Hey Kid, how are you doing?" His demeanor being so fitting and human for someone who would be fetching a child, I looked at this entity and pondered who and what they were. At that point, I noticed that the sun coming in through the Living-room windows was showing through what was actually a pair of integrated goggles on what was like a Hazmat suit that this being was wearing. The eyes underneath reminded me of an owl's.

Once again, I have an in-between memory where I was standing in the front room with these "Grey's" in their bio-suits, three or four of them. The one who crawled in behind the easy-chairs to fetch me is handed a device that I recall as looking remarkably similar to an old-fashion RC controller for model air-planes. If it's not an over-lay, it's a remarkable coincidence that their technology would appear so similar to an aspect of my Grand-father's interest in aviation. I ended up asking if and how we'd be leaving, I could sense the leader smiling as he telepathically responded "Through the Window."

"How," I sent back. I really wanted to know I guess, perhaps still remembering the previous encounter and being floated out the window on some level.

"You'll see," was the calm and measured response.

This was different from the blue-white light from the winter's evening before. It was as though the light of the Sun itself became solid as it emanated through the window and pulled me through it, much more fast and immediate.

I'm not sure what happened during that incident either and in fact, I don't have much in the way of recall of what was done with me on board ship, I felt extremely groggy and unpleasant after that encounter.

One other probable experience that happened at my grandparent's house came back to me in a dream. When the family home was bulldozed and a new double-wide put in, we stayed with my grandparents.

While I was walking through the kitchen I felt

myself being pulled forward by some invisible force. My feet floated off the ground as I moved towards the door. Mother was there and asked me what was happening. I told her: "I can't stop it, something is moving me." I was then carried through the foyer and out the front door. To my mother's credit, she did try to hold on to me as I was pulled into the air towards this immense white yellowish light hovering over the driveway. I remember being lifted into the air towards the light and my conscious memory of what happened fades around that point.

There are not many more definite abduction related experiences that I recall from my youth, another that occurred of interest was the time I was a little boy out playing in the sand-box in the front yard with Mom. Abruptly, it was like the air just changed and she announced that she had to go into the house but for me to go ahead and wait for her, Once she left, I felt compelled to lay down on the ground and I saw the legs of entities standing near me. Then being floated up on my back through the upper boughs of tall pine-trees that overlooked the front-yard. I looked above me and saw a classic silvery disc with what appeared to be a black, circular opening in the bottom.

Another interesting incident occurred when I was so young that I can barely remember how old I was. I was actually shown a kind of cartoon-like vision concerning my mother, the issues she would face in life and how it could affect her aging. I saw her as an archetypically happy little girl dressed all in bows and ribbons and bonneted dress, even carrying a basket, skipping down a forest path. I saw her become mired in quick-sand.

To get back to lost artifacts, somewhere, there might still be an image I took of the Deering Public Library, in the image you can see a metallic orb hanging almost directly over one of the spires on this ornate building. I've been given a multitude of signs and explanation of my affiliation with and this level of interaction with space-faring intelligences.

There is a fair deal of fear and trauma mixed in with these interactions, especially through my teen years; insomnia and compounded neurosis is a common feature due to the aspect of feeling used by beings with very different understandings of physicality. Or who view us as a resource. As noted, I do not have full recall of events that occurred on ship, one of the problems I've had is that their sexual-mores are markedly different from ours. I remember waking up one morning crying and even though I didn't remember what had happened, I felt violated.

Years later and once again, in Nevada, I had a flash-back of being on my back with female entity straddling me. This sexual aspect is yet another element showing that we are dealing with a common source for what experiencers report. It's also worth noting that it is in keeping with the Lustful aspect ascribed to those who travelled to and from the Stars. The narrative of cosmic-life is becoming more bound by light as we realize that this is what we truly want. Yet I still find myself considering that epic moments or sequences in our incarnations are driven by their inherent value and glory towards the collective identity of us as Beings with a rich and compelling history.

Of course, our interactions with these other People not bound Planet-side are more complicated than simply saying that we are being exploited or either that we have always been treated with the level of regard and concern that we would expect and rightly demand. It would seem that the consciousness of these being is torn between sensitivity and a perspective that does not see intelligence as being separate like ours does. Therefore, if they see something as being for a greater good, they will commit to it with a shocking determination and automatic routine. What is under this however?

In the case of the one whom I have come to refer to as Egerie Nocturne after a revealing ballad composed in Occitan: What stands out for me are the impression I had wasn't so much that she didn't care that her forcing herself on me was putting me under duress. It was an eagerness for the sensations involved that she sought out because they were something she saw as preferable and therefore something worth acting upon rather than not.

Yet the desire was motivated by an incredibly deep and complex need. It conveyed an impression of being confronted by someone wanting intimacy that had fallen in Love with someone and found them unable to resist their impulses. That may seem vain but keep in mind; this was not a gratifying experience. Plus, as aforementioned, there are other Experiencers who recount such sexual interactions occurring between them and Non-Earth-Bounders. -Although, let's keep in mind that we can Astral-travel off planet and affirming that we are still having Arrivals and Departures to and from the Vastness of other Abodes above is part of the reason why individuals such as me have come forward in the first place.

Point being, this is a part of the experience that we admit too with some reluctance and part of that is because we are afraid of pre-planned accusations that we have screen memories or psychological afflictions that render us prone to fantasizing about being singled out in this way. On one hand, it can become something empowering but like any lengthy and drastic pattern of Life there are things you wish would have gone smoother with less scattering.

As I have integrated the reality of these on-going events however, my awareness of them has changed for the better just as others report. I am now in a state of near open contact with related beings and others, a claim for which I have evidence for in the form of numerous amounts of film-footage and images. I find this revelation cathartic and vindicating.

To spare the recounting of encounters for a few paragraphs: The manner in which this has been conveyed to me involves synchronicity of events and locations. Simply but aptly put, synchronicity is one of the ways in which higher-intelligences with the ability to create such events: Communicates with us.

This is a multi-dimensional modality of not just communication but establishing a coordinate in Space-time and frequency. As they are bound by the focal-resonance of a location, so are those loci enhanced in ability to access and establish an interaction there. This is how Cosmic-energies are linked with Pyramids, part of their power or drive-chain is in drawing in observation and applying that to an alignment that leads into Cosmic-knowledge. This is one of the highest inclusive insights in archaic wisdom. You know the phrase "As Above, So Below."?

In this case, although we need to take the blessing with thought, the richness is shown by the individual experience that resonates with those who share in it and that are why I write this account. For me personally, there is a focal-point featuring the name Putnam.
The Phoenix Lights are a solid case for contact with an advanced civilization. Yet comparatively little attention is given to a wave of sightings in the Hudson Valley region of New York primarily throughout the early 1980's but also for years after. The craft described and caught on film had remarkable similarities with the Phoenix Craft.

A majority of these sightings occurred in association with Putnam County. While this was going on, during the early 1980's and around the same time that I was conceived: My mother and Grandmother encountered one of these craft on one of those quintessential, historic sections of New-England back-roads. It cruised up over a mountain and went past them. This occurred on Old Putnam hill road.

Looking back, I can feel that I was on-board that ship, recounting previous incarnations and gearing up for this one. No one has a wholly Earth-bound identity but I can consider the contacts I've had in my life and how I came to be here for confirmation that I am a more recent arrival.

It would seem that my heritage is strongly Lyran in essence from what I have been told and had indicated by the craft piloted over the Earth matching the massive flying "^" form, some examples in Belgium were documented on Radar clocking in at speeds and making maneuvers that showed intelligent control but at speeds that -as has become typically observed in cases- give the Bird to dictated definitions of physics.

In a Dream-vision, I watched a flotilla of bright silver discs with reddish light emanating from the bottom descends down the road from me. Whereupon I was approached by a crowd of People, one of which told me "They've landed, they're Tall Blondes! You're one of them!"

This is one of those things I try to keep my ego in check over.

Yet, on the other hand, I find myself considering that we do need to recognize and honor our blessings. Not from the stand-point of holding others inferior and this should go without saying. It's not even something gratifying for the Ego, ultimately, as to follow through means taking responsibility. Auditing who you have been and allowing that to show you what is desirable and what you must release and purge. People become infected by this and deny it, covering over the wound so that it never heals and has an effect on how they relate to others holistically.

It is in the spirit and intention of clearing out such infectious material from this Planet and any residue from the active aspect of the Hall of Records that I share this account of my perspective on my encounters for this volume and any who read it. May you be blessed with knowing that you are a stellar and singular eminence that holds a brilliant light.

Korey Lavoie ~ Bio

Korey Lavoie is a life-long contactee and researcher who combines extensive study with his own higher-faculties to produce insights and realizations that have helped him to further understand himself and that he also hopes can be of use too others.

Korey divides his time between volunteering and acting as a writer, researcher and experiential presenter of information and documentation relevant to applied esoteric concepts and Paradigm enhancing knowledge. Fleet Activity

Currently, he is engaged in furthering his own contact, sharing the results and taking a step forward with intent to engage in offering what he can to teach others as a lecturer, advisor and Healer.

Mr. Lavoie integrates a vast number of concepts and recognizes phenomenon as occurring on a Holistic basis where non-biased scientific knowledge continuously supports and reforms aspects of verifiable, experienced esoterica and contact with non-terrestrially bound intelligence.

One might say that his purpose in having incarnated here is as a Volunteer; a title he holds with pride."

Korey Lavoie was born in 1983 in New England at the same time that The Hudson Valley wave of sightings was occurring in upstate New-York. Growing up, he faced many personal challenges, yet during this time, there was intercession and interaction in his life from Non-human entities. In his own estimation, many of these events are typical for experiencers.

However, he recognizes that each recounting of such events brings us all a broader perspective on such interactions: He finds that he can bring a unique and highly integrated perspective to such events and information that he has acquired in the course of his own extensive study of this and related phenomenon as well as multitudinous shared insights into our true Nature as Cosmic beings and citizens in an inhabited Solar-System.

The nature of our relationship to them and his contacts have taught him about the nature of the fathoms of energy that we inhabit and how this is being gradually integrated by our Celestial family with our help.

BEYOND THE SPACE-TIME CONTINUUM: WHERE AM I?
Rebecca Hardcastle Wright, Ph.D.

What we think as time/space...is a relative thing. Our appearance, reality and identity are relative and different according to the relative point of view. Einstein describes something known in all the worlds' spiritual and magical traditions—the identity, reality, and location of the human being are something relative. R.J. Stewart

Veins of coal run through West Virginia. Men and women enter elevators that drop into the underground, the underworld. My ancestors, German-Scot-Irish, were independent souls who settled West Virginia and mined those veins. Their stubborn independence roots them to the land and the underground long after it is financially or physically viable. What force keeps them living in poverty above abandoned mines?

What secrets do the hills and hollows keep?

In Arizona, Native American reservations are portals to other worlds. Underworld creatures inhabit these portals. These creatures are painted in story and pottery—serpent, spider, corn-mother, lizard.

In West Virginia, backwoods communities and generations of close families secure the portals to other worlds--underworlds inhabited by creatures of story, song, quilt, and craft.

As an adolescent, I recall sitting in a junior high gymnasium in Buckhannon, West Virginia, eating a brown bag lunch on the bleachers. Every school has an industrial smell, probably sanitizing solvents. Whatever it is, it infiltrates your nose memory during childhood. The school smell is stimulated by pervasive, lifeless, institutional green paint.

This school had a particularly pungent smell—rich, fetid, earthy. Gymnasium sweat mingled with childhood lunch aromas. It was a consolidated school system and some of my classmates walked miles out of the mountains to catch a bus, only to start another lengthy journey to school. They were paid a penny a mile to walk to catch the bus.

Next to me on the bleachers sat a young girl. She rode a school bus home to another world deep within the mountains. Our school was in a small college town that offered planned activities for teenagers she never experienced. Every afternoon her bus crossed the town limits and she entered the foreign space of mountain culture.

During lunch, she related how her mother encountered a snake prior to her brother's birth. Walking into the barn, a snake coiled in front of her and rose to strike.

Belly full with child, she ran safely back to the house. When her brother came into the world with a large serpentine birth mark their family and community understood the importance. Her brother was marked. Her eyes widened as she repeated his fate. Her brother was marked.

I did not understand marking. I did not understand mountain life. I did not understand stories of carrying a rifle through the woods on a Friday night to go 'coon hunting. It was more than my adolescent mind could fathom. Yet, her endless stories struck a chord in me. She knew something I knew. Signs carry meaning. Animals communicate information.

Mountain culture of the underworld is off limits. It is off limits to technology and the media. It is off limits to strangers. It is blanketed, secreted away. As a child I stumbled into the underworld and fell below into another dimension. Then I forgot the experience and trekked my way into adulthood. I forgot until, as an adult, the serpent reappeared in Scottsdale, Arizona, claiming that the underworld wanted me back. I could have ignored its invitation. There was no insistence. It simply seemed natural to accept. With the serpent's invitation, I began living in parallel realities above and below.

I maintained my family, job, and friends, while experiencing conscious visitations by creatures who seemed more suitable for Saturday morning cartoons.

These creatures are inhabitants of what I call the underworld dimension. Other cultures and other researchers may use another term. I choose the term underworld because of my vivid childhood memory of coming up from and out of its invisible boundary.

Creatures of the underworld dimension are primarily reptilian. They are large, sometimes seven to eight foot standing reptiles. I can "feel" their dry scaly skin.

Sometimes their skin reflects a glowing iridescent light. I sense their powerful and purposeful energy. I discriminate between them—male, female, familiar, stranger. They appear and hover just outside my conscious mind until I communicate. They seem to inhabit a world within our world, a dimension just outside our reality.

Other creatures from the underworld appear as serpents, standing snakes. They too are large beings. Like reptiles, these serpents communicate with me. Are they the Old Testament Garden of Eden variety of serpent? Perhaps. They seem capable of wisdom and healing.

Accompanying the reptiles and serpents are gentle, wise, praying mantis type creatures. Tall, thin, angular, limbed creatures, they constantly move with a gentle motion. Their elbow joints open and close as they manifest. Huge dark eyes wrap around narrow heads. They feel shy, with a startling intellect, wisdom, and knowledge.

As my ability to communicate with these creatures increased, so did the frequency of our contact. A relationship ensued. A trust developed. I understood that I was dealing with a dimension known to many of my ancestors.

It was a dimension hidden and forgotten, or perhaps shunned and ignored for fear of persecution. The experience of my ancestors was probably no different than the Irish who talk of the fairies and leprechauns, who pop out of the ground to play with children in the garden and woodlands. Only I didn't see cute fairies in childhood, I saw seven and eight foot creatures. That's a "big" difference.

Fortunately, my underworld experience was authenticated by relationships I was forming in Arizona. A friend introduced me to an internationally eminent anomalous researcher, Dr. Ruth Hover. She became my mentor and friend. If there was a Native American, alternative history or UFO book, Dr. Ruth had read it and added it to her library. Active in researching anomalous phenomenon since the 1950s, she had ties to many of the post-war research institutes. To this day, she maintains an impressive global network of fellow researchers who trust her scientific mind, archival memory, and network of colleagues.

I joined Dr. Ruth's monthly "contact group." It was composed of professional people, parents, and young adults, united through their extraterrestrial contact experience.

The group was the first place I found acceptance and calm acknowledgement of my experiences. Everyone was on the same frequency. None were afraid or panic stricken by their contact. It was a fact of their life.

Luckily, I found Dr. Ruth's group before I found David Icke's books. In ufology there are individuals, like Icke, who vilify reptilian underworld energies. They link them to the Illuminati, to shape-shifters, to evil manipulators of wealth and the desire for a domineering world government. They link them to the cabal and the secret government. They cloak all purported reptilian experiences to conspiracy.

Eager for any reptilian information, I read David Icke's books. I respect his research and experiences. But, they are not mine. And yet, I agree with many of his conclusions. No doubt, as Icke maintains, reality is not what we deem it to be. My dimensional experiences validated that. No doubt the wealthy gather to network privately, set agendas, and make decisions. This seemed a probable political reality. No doubt, certain individuals shape shift to reveal another nature. Shamans make a habit of it when they astral travel. No doubt reptilian energy is ancient and difficult to comprehend.

No doubt individuals in our government and military know of these underworlds, reptilian energies and perhaps work with them. Icke demonized the reptilian underworld dimension and those who associated with and misused its energies. As I lived with these energies, critical judgments faded.

Reptilians are real. They dwell in another dimension. They can be communicated with and related to. They can be respected and trusted. They provide and maintain an active inter-dimensional portal. Re-entering this portal in adulthood, I experienced their reality with a mature perspective. Reptilian reality threads through human reality, it manifests in Bible stories, myths, legends, and art. Reptilian reality anchors human reality. Through them, earth secrets are revealed. Through them, earth structures are maintained and protected.

As I reacquainted with the underworld, I began to uncover ancient wisdom—sacred geometry, number, vibration, energy. My earth citizenship as a "crust dweller" expanded into deep levels of esoteric knowledge. Like a rabbit transfixed by a snake, I shifted into altered states of consciousness where the fabric of life had a different texture.

Architecture and structure became a science of proportion and beauty. Viewing exquisite buildings triggered a deep sense of satisfaction, a familiar vibration. Agriculture and its seasons of sowing seeds, then nurturing plants to harvest expanded into the esoteric science of crop circles. Throughout the world, but primarily in Avebury, Stonehenge, and Silbury Hill, England, crop circles appear in late summer, just prior to harvest. They imprint the earth with geometric, mathematical symbols for the eager initiate to decipher using science and metaphysics. Every summer new messages appear on the surface of the earth.

Through the reptilian lens, art and myth focus. Story is reality. Whether it was ancient myths like Isis and Osiris, or Persephone in the underworld, or Jason and the Golden Fleece, each of these stories ring true as the reality of the underworld. Yes, humans journey through the portal of the underworld and return to tell of their adventure.

All humans journey through the underworld, either conscious or unconscious. The choice is yours. Being human, you possess a cord to underworld environs. You can travel the cord—awake or asleep. Once the blindfold is removed, you have the ability to travel and encounter an inter-dimensional underworld community.

Eyes open, aware, you can choose to view the underworld as demonic, cruel, and controlling. There are many like Icke who share this view. If it were up to them, everyone would cut the cord and be free of the underworld. You would then reject the human reality of the underworld perceived as controlling and dangerous.

Or, eyes open, aware, you can choose to view the underworld as simply another dimension to explore and consciously inhabit. To do this, you need to suspend judgment and expectations. Then, you can learn to navigate its terrain, and in so doing, learn about yourself and earth dimensions.

Eyes open, aware, the underworld becomes one among multiple dimensions. Reptilian reality becomes one of many dimensional realities inhabited with intelligent beings. Human, living on planet earth, you begin to see yourself as part of an inter-dimensional reality.

Bring on the underworld myths, they no longer frighten. Bring on the hideous monsters; they no longer lurk in the dark. Bring on the next visit, you know you will easily return, wiser and more mature. It is not a matter of conquering the underworld dimension. It is not a matter of denying the underworld dimension. It is not a matter of demonizing the underworld dimension. Instead, it is simply a matter of owning the part of your human nature that is corded to its reality. In so doing, ancient knowledge, once secret and forbidden, opens to reveal its simplicity and truth.

Ancient underworld knowledge includes innate human abilities to sense earth vibrations, to find your way on the earth using psychic sense. Celtic tradition tells of blindfolding children, leaving them like Hansel and Gretel in the woods. Parents trusted the child's psychic earth-centered abilities to find their way home. Have you ever traveled and found your way without compass or stars? That ability may be linked to your innate underworld abilities.

As global warming intensifies and earth changes move over populations like a tidal wave, underworld wisdom leads the way to protection and safety. Like reptiles, humans may need to burrow to survive. Underworld energies protect and maintain the structure of planet earth. Underworld wisdom is ancient and timely. Have you ever sensed an impending earthquake or storm? That ability may be linked to your innate underworld abilities. Intuitively, you know when it is time to take cover.

Your relation to the underworld is simple and yet complex. At one point I discovered that beings in the underworld dimension, like humans, were open to realigning relationships. After years of communication with reptilians and other underworld beings and energies, I felt it was time to move on. I needed to reorder the relationship. I needed to put some detachment and distance between us.

I wanted to respect our lines of communication, yet I needed to detach from their energies. And so, I simply requested that we reconfigure our relationship. We dialogued for several days and then we realigned. I have a vivid memory of declaring to them that the time of my initiation and education was over. Our intense time, almost like a courtship, had ended. I wanted to communicate and relate to them on different terms. We negotiated, and then agreed.

Reptilians still appear and communicate. I travel to the underworld, though less frequently. I honor our relationship and the energy we share. They are intimately connected to our earth dimension. I know that somehow—through DNA or bloodline or frequency—I am connected to them. That may never change. What did change was my naïve perspective of who I am and how I shape my reality. I shape my reality through respect and knowledge, not through fear. I acknowledge myself as an inter-dimensional being—not a flatlander of three dimensions. I thank reptilians for this orientation and wisdom.

REPTILIAN LEGACY TO THE STARS

Confusing questions rise when links appear between dimensions. Connectedness is fraught with questions. How does the reptilian underworld correlate with extraterrestrials?

If I cord to the underworld do I also cord to the stars and inter-galactic dimensions? Yes, underworld, cosmic and earth dimensions are inter-related, interconnected. Your human legacy is the underworld and the stars. Many extraterrestrial contactees witness alien cosmic grey type beings working alongside underworld reptilian beings. For example, Jim Sparks, an abductee interviewed by journalist, Linda Moulton Howe in her book Glimpses of Other Realities, Vol II reported an underworld visitation with extraterrestrial components.

While living in North Carolina and working in real estate development, Jim had a series of encounters. Awakened in the middle of the night by a low-pitched whirling sound, he felt himself pulled down. Then he became aware of being transported through the wall and on to a craft. In the craft, he identified small alien grays as workers, tall aliens as supervisors, and tall reptoids with scaly reptile skin as overseers. On board the craft, during a series of encounters, Jim learned to decipher alien symbols and language.

He reported learning to read from right to left, bottom to top, seeing three dimensional letters and symbols. He claims he could feel and see the words.

Similar to Jim Sparks' contact experience, our human origins are linked to underworld and cosmic dimensions that seem to co-exist with our earth life of three dimensions plus time. And yet, many in the scientific research community scoff at alternative researchers eager to explore cosmic and underworld dimensions.

Researchers studying our possible extraterrestrial origins are currently on a divergent research tangent, largely ignored by the scientific community. Few mainline researchers embrace the possibility of human connection and legacy to dimensional realities. Most extraterrestrial, underworld research remains independent. Yet, despite the exclusion, a growing number of independent researchers are opening the door to important information. These independent researchers are trained academic scholars who hold themselves to high research standards, regardless of the present separation from their academic community. Due to their research commitment and public communication, information on our possible extraterrestrial origins is becoming widely available.

The godfather of extraterrestrial origins research is Zecharia Sitchin, a Biblical scholar knowledgeable in modern and ancient Hebrew, Old Testament, Semitic, and European languages. Sitchin researched ancient Sumerian documents for 30 years prior to the publication of The Twelfth Planet in 1976.

According to Sitchin, Sumer, which was biblical Shin'ar, was situated on the plain between the Tigris and Euphrates, site of current-day Iraq. This ancient civilization held knowledge of the full solar system with all outer planets, including Uranus, discovered in 1781, Neptune, discovered in 1846, and Pluto, discovered in 1930. The Sumerian story of the planet Earth's creation is that when Planet Nibiru, ("Planet of the Crossing" or "Planet X") entered our solar system, one of its moons collided with planet Tiamat, breaking it in two. One segment exploded into an asteroid belt and one segment emerged as planet Earth.

Planet Nibiru, according to the Sumerians and Sitchin, is on a large elliptical orbit that brings it into our solar system between Mars and Jupiter every 3,600 years. Its arrival is announced with comet-like tail ancients called the "seed of life."

Sitchin's research also uncovered evidence of our human origins linked to the Annunaki, a race whose home planet was Nibiru. This same Annunaki race is linked to underworld reptilians and controlling Illuminati factions of conspiracy theory. According to Sitchin, the extraterrestrial, and later Earth dwelling and underworld Annunaki beings created humans by a carefully conceived union of their DNA with the most advanced human life form on earth at the time. According to Sitchin, Sumerian records cite the creation of advanced humans by the Annunaki for the purpose of mining gold and working as slaves. (No wonder the veins of West Virginia hold their secrets.)

Despite the fact that immortality was not granted this hybrid human, these hybrid humans caused no end of grief for the Annunaki. The Sumerian documents relate a decision by an angered Enlil, one of the Annunaki leaders, to cause a global catastrophic flood and weather upheavals to wipe the troublesome hybrid human off the face of the earth.

The Epic of Gilgamesh tells the story of another Annunaki, Enki, who was dedicated to protecting humans, against his angry elder brother's wishes. Enki instructed select humans to build a vessel to survive the floods. Of course, this flood story is retold in many versions throughout the world. The best known to the Western world is the Old Testament Noah story. This seems an obvious retelling of the Epic of Gilgamesh.

A primary religious resource for mainstream Sunday sermons and biblical teaching, The Interpreter's Bible, briefly references the Sumerian and Babylonians as the basis of the Old Testament. According to Fretheim, a contributor in the Genesis volume, "Israel drew on a widespread fund of images and ideas to shape into a creation story."

He cites the similarity of the Old Testament creation story with Babylonian Enuma Elis, the Epic of Atrahasis, and the Egyptian creation account that emphasized "the word."

Then he cites dissimilarities between the Old Testament and the Sumerian Babylonian creation. According to Fretheim, the Old Testament account differs distinctly from the Sumerian Babylonian. The Old Testament account lacks: a) Theogony (listing of Gods), b) conflict among the Gods, and c) prevailing monotheism. Similarities between the Old Testament and Babylonia creation include: a) images of God as a potter, working with existing materials, b) God fighting with and achieving victory over chaotic forces.

Eventually, research of ancient sources, aided by technology advances, will weave the slender threads separating creation stories. A holistic, integrated retelling of creation allows humans a clearer understanding of who we are, and where we came from, in order to move forward.

Will Hart in The Genesis Race: Our Extraterrestrial DNA and the True Origins of the Species researches the creation stories of the Old Testament, uncovering a possible extraterrestrial presence. According to Hart, the two creation stories, Genesis 1 and 2 present divergent creation stories. Genesis 1 outlines the familiar seven days of creation and Genesis 2 outlines the creation of man from dust and the Garden of Eden. Citing both creation stories, Hart points to the confusion between Yahweh, one God, creating man in his own image and Elohim, or the plural "Let us make man in our image" (The New Oxford Annotated Bible, Gen.1.26). Whether the God of creation is singular or plural,

Genesis reflects an almost human nature on to our creator. Genesis 3.8 refers to the "sound of the Lord walking in the Garden." Genesis 3.9 refers to the Lord calling to man "Where are you?" The Lord then makes a garment for Adam and Eve. Genesis 6.2 tells what happened when the "sons of God saw the daughters of man." These scriptures are often used to refer to the race of giants or the Nephilim who occupied Earth.

Finally Hart refers to the human nature of angelic appearances in the Old Testament as another indication of extraterrestrial origins. In Genesis 19, Lot is sitting at the gates of Sodom as the Angels approach. They go to Lot's house where they eat and speak. Hart asserts that Old Testament Angels and God(s) of creation who walk and talk may be extraterrestrial beings. Talking, walking, sewing, reproducing all indicate that the

God(s) of the Old Testament had human-like qualities and abilities. Hart indicates that the ancient storytellers were describing our extraterrestrial ancestors who also may have been instrumental in our creation.

The Dead Sea Scrolls and Nag Hammadi, additional source documents of the Old Testament, also provide information on our possible extraterrestrial origins. The Dead Sea Scrolls contain fragments of the books of Enoch in Aramaic.

Enoch was known as the first among the "children of men" born on the Earth with knowledge of writing, science, and wisdom from the Angels. According to Andrew Collins in his book, From the Ashes of Angels, Watchers are a specific divine race of Angels, "meaning those who watch or those who are awake." These Watchers are Angels sent from the Lord.

They come down to Earth to instruct humans to bring about justice and equality. Enoch travels to heaven to meet with the Angels to testify about the interbreeding among Watchers and humans. Punishment was determined to come by flooding the Earth.

The creation story of the Nag Hammadi describes the bodies of Adam and Eve as overlaid with horny skin that was bright as daylight, like a luminescent garment, such that they didn't need clothing. The description of Adam and Eve's skin sounds reptilian.

In an article in Fate Magazine, Joe Lewels describes the Garden of Eden encounter of these reptilian beings. As Adam and Eve ate from the tree of knowledge, "She took some of its fruit and ate, and she gave to her husband also…then their minds opened. For when they ate, the light of knowledge shone for them. When they saw their makers, they loathed them since they were beastly forms. They understood very much."

These biblical source documents creation stories reference a possible extraterrestrial superhuman reptilian race involved in human creation. Contemporary scientists concur. Neurologists cite the vestiges of human reptilian heritage in the core of the human brain.

The R-complex or reptilian complex is responsible for aggressive behavior, territoriality, ritual, and social hierarchies. The middle brain, or limbic system, represents the human mammalian heritage. This part of the brain is responsible for feelings of love, hate, compassion, and sentimentality. The outer layer of the brain or the neo-cortex is responsible for reasoning, deliberation, and the place where we determine the difference between good and evil.

As ancient biblical source documents are examined using technology and as lost books become accessible, our extraterrestrial lineage may become more apparent and less threatening. Our concept of God(s) may need to readjust and broaden as the reality of our divine maker emerges. Those familiar with research concerning our extraterrestrial origins are forging new territory, characterizing certain behaviors and attributes as "star seed." As details about our creators emerge, human extraterrestrial-like abilities become commonplace. Like our creators, we see ourselves moving naturally among dimensions as telepathic, psychic, vibration beings that can teleport and time travel.

Rebecca Hardcastle Wright, PhD ~ Bio

Rebecca Hardcastle Wright, PhD, is the founder of the Institute for Exoconsciousness. The Institute's mission is to support ET Experiencers through research and application of the innate ability of human consciousness to connect and communicate with ETs. The Institute builds bridges between ET experiencers and consciousness science as well as connects ET experiencers with international experiencer groups.

Rebecca's signature is exploring what it means to be an Exoconscious Human, how we form an ET identity. She authored *Exoconsciousness: Your 21st Century Mind*. Rebecca teaches Exoconsciousness at International Metaphysical University. Formerly, she was a member of Dr. Edgar Mitchell's Quantrek international science team, researching zero point energy, consciousness, and the ET Presence. In 2005 Rebecca taught one of the first ufology courses in the nation at Scottsdale Community College in Arizona.

www.exoconsciousness.com

Exoconsciousness: Your 21st Century Mind

THE STORY OF JOAN OF ANGELS

Joan Hangarter, DC

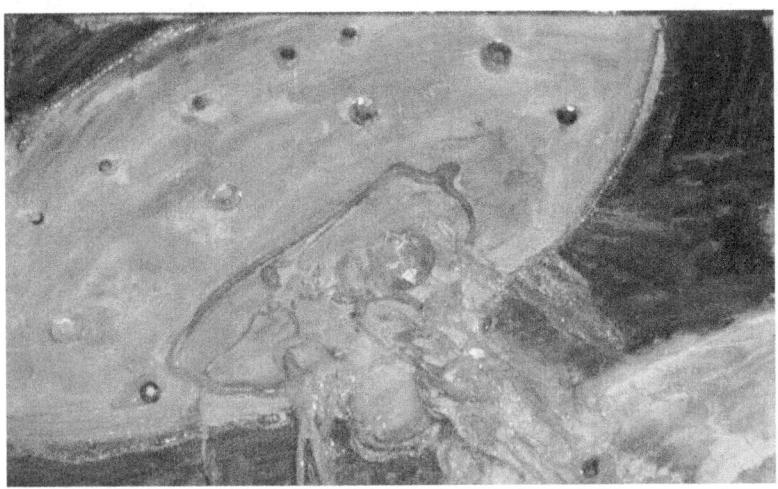

Fall of 2010; as my youngest child is leaving for college, our family home is going into foreclosure. Change is in the air, and with some trepidation I pack up the house, and move to Baja California, a vast land with blue skies and a history of UFO and ET encounters. The story that caught my interest of an ET landing in the center of the tiny fishing village of San Felipe compels me forward.

Acting from a sense of destiny, I found a group named Baja Paranormal Research Association and begin holding monthly meetings, hoping to satisfy my curiosity. People from the surrounding areas arrive at the meetings with photos of their latest UFO sightings from right down the street. The sky is often filled with clusters of strange saucer shaped clouds sitting directly overhead, stationary for hours at a time.

My dreams are vivid; I see spaceships landing in my yard, beckoning me, as the portal doors are open and I am drawn inward. These dreams of spaceships fill my mind 24/7 and soon I am painting what I am sensing in my dreams.

One night I am sure I am dreaming. I wake up and find myself on a small, saucer shaped ship, just like the ones I've been seeing regularly as clouds, and I know intuitively this ship is one of six or seven smaller ships connected to a large mothership high over Baja. As I look around the room we are in, I realize I am the only one awake; I am in a room filled with the members of my group, but they are all sound asleep, in a trance.

I am standing on a raised platform off to one corner of the room. One by one, the sleeping people are brought to me, and placed in a chair. I am tuning up their antenna, that's my job. I understand my mission, my destiny, is to tune up, raise the frequency of, and properly align all the people on this planet, adjusting their vibration to resonate in harmony and balance with the rest of the sentient beings and Mother Earth herself.

I am informed that once every sentient being has their frequency aligned, and then Gaia, just as an orchestra, will be in tune, in harmony, in balance so she can sing her son, the song of the Earth, the song of the blue planet. Once that happens, we, as a collective will ascend to our next levels.

That's what I am doing, one person at a time, standing on a platform in a scout like saucer ship connected to a mother ship, knowing I am to tune up the entire world population, not one soul to be lost. The enormity of my task causes me to scream out, surprising myself. *"Are you kidding, one person at a time, this will take forever!"*

At this moment in direct answer to my prayers, two people appear on the ship, my dear friend Shima Moore, program director at Conscious Life Expo and another man, a telecommunications/scalar technology wiz. I was informed they would be my support team. Apparently, my mission was just beginning, and I wouldn't be alone.

Several months passed and I move to Arizona, to

continue my studies of UFO and landing sights. The area and specifically even the house where I am staying is a known hotbed for inter-dimensional and UFO activity, lying directly in the path of the UFO Highway.

Several times each week, I excitedly notice orbs in the back by the mountains, flying up and down, horizontal, disappearing and reappearing where no lights should be. The house is a portal of some type. On the evenings when the orbs are sighted, videos capture orbs so large and dense they often obscure my car, so it can't be seen in the video recordings.

The house attracts Ascended Masters, ET's, angels and departed loved ones. I live for these frequent encounters with their presences for it confirms to me these experiences are real. Occasionally one of these beings tries to speak with me, to get my attention, and to download information. I love being able to easily slip from this dimension to theirs within this portal.

One night, I awaken from a deep sleep; as I open my eyes, I see is a group of five or six tall, beautiful, illuminated, brightly lit, silvery beings encircling me, round and round, sending me healing energies. I watch them with my eyes open, and as I close my eyes, they are still with me. I'm not afraid, in fact I get up again during the night, walk outside, see a spaceship, and go back to bed, still feeling and seeing their presence around me.

The next morning, I attend an event in southern California, Portal to Ascension. Much to my surprise, as I enter the main room, there, on a table, is a collection of ET sculptures of every variety, sculpted by Cynthia Crawford, the ET sculptor. On the table is an exact replica of the silvery beings I had seen and felt the night before.

Per Cynthia, I was visited by the "teachers", a group of beings that were downloading very specific information. These beings were coming to me and sharing their wisdom, so that that one day, I might share the knowledge with the rest of humanity. I am being prepared to become a channel, a carrier and transmitter of this ancient wisdom.

That night, I take home a tall white extraterrestrial representation of the white Zeta's. From the moment, I bring him home, I realize he is a living sentient being of some sort, with a vast intelligence and telepathic skills. Almost immediately, I received his downloads, packets of information revealing to me that I am a *"galactic ambassador"* of some type, here to assist and work with humanity and their connection with the extra-terrestrial and the galactic council.

That was the beginning of an intense period of channeling for me. It seemed that even without knowing someone I could sense their destiny, their mission, and where they came from, why they were here. In fact, I couldn't stop myself.

My life in 2013 was quite stressful and unsettled, and I asked my guides, I literally prayed that if I couldn't manifest the destiny I knew was mine, to take my life. Instead, a series of events led me to host a painting party on Halloween evening, and at the time, I began receiving instructions to paint 33 angels in 30 days.

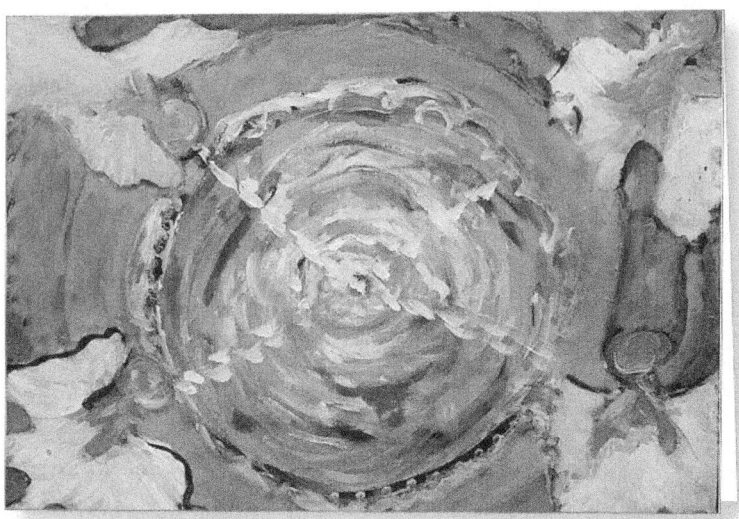

It was like I was hearing an intense pressure in my right ear, along with a sense of paint, Joan, paint. Paint 33 angels in 30 days, just do it, don't question, do it and more will be revealed. Thus, I began 30 days in a state of intense connection to spirit, painting angels, departed loved ones, spirit guides; they all came rushing through me to be put on a canvas. I was a whirling dervish with a paintbrush in hand. I could close my eyes and paint, turn the canvas upside down, it didn't matter. I was merely the paintbrush for spirit.

Thirty days later, I hung up all the art in what became the angel loft. As I look around and ask out loud, okay, what now, a book fell off the bookshelf. I had carried this paperback with me for years, never reading it. The title, invoking your celestial guardian angel was more than appropriate and so was the page that had opened.

"Your call for divine assistance has been heard." I was guided to continue painting. "Paint us and we will come," was what I heard along with the information that many people had received the instructions to paint 33 angels in 30 days, but few had chosen to do it, except for me. I read that day, *"If you are to be one of the chosen ones, you must choose."*

Now, I live in my Desert Heart Sanctuary in the Coachella Valley area, where I paint divine beings, celestials and star beings, as well as portals, stargates and ascension chambers. The energy and the information of what to paint, comes in packets of information, downloads, and I find myself painting in almost a trance.

These beings have a name overall, as the earth messengers: beings sent by the divine to assist humanity. They tell me they come to me to paint, so humans can experience them in the 3-d world, on a canvas, a physical sighting so to speak. I send the paintings wherever they are needed for healing, and the reports I receive are astounding. These paintings themselves are packages of healing, loving, information for people.

Within a day of receiving instructions to move to the desert here so I can hear the ETS and angels, I was named by anew friend, Joan of Angels. Yay,…..

Joan of Angels, AKA Dr. Joan Hangarter, DC

Joan Hangarter, DC ~ Bio

Joan of Angels (also known as Dr. Joan Hangarter, DC) is a visionary, intuitive artist, consultant and life coach, healer, author, and speaker, who have dedicated her life to learning the art of manifesting miracles and living your dreams. Joan is the founder of The Miracle Makers Club and Desert Heart Angel Sanctuary where she assists people in remembering who they are, why they are here and how to fulfill their destiny. She courageously assists you to call in your vision, clear your obstacles and renew your courage to follow your callings and, hear what your guides and angels want you to know now.

In 2013, artist Dr. Joan Hangarter heard the call of the Earth Messengers, *'Paint us and we will come."* Dr. Hangarter had been a successful chiropractor, an author and founder of The Miracle Makers Club. But in 2013, she dropped everything and began to paint transformative paintings of angels she calls Earth Messengers, Beings Sent by the Divine.

"The Earth Messengers are here to bring healing of the heart, and remind us, that we, too, are powerful beings with the potential to live a larger life. The process of painting these Earth Messengers begins with a vision, a dream, and through a meditative process, the paint brush literally moves itself, and the beings direct their presentation."

Her paintings are imbued with positive transformational messages from etheric beings that Dr. Joan shares as she channels as an oracle, medium and a painter—earning her the affectionate moniker '*Joan of Angels.*'

Joan of Angels has recently begun to share her work as an oracle and speaker. *"The message of 'Paint us and we will come,' is part of a universal truth for all of us, with a larger theme of believe, and your truth, your life, will manifest."*

Joan of Angels is available for personal or group readings and channeled messages. Make an appointment for a reading with Joan or view her art and work at http://www.joanofangels.com/

Joan of Angels Messenger for the Divine: Raising your vibrational frequency to create positive change!
www.joanofangels.com, 415-717-1385
www.joanofangels.com

NEAR DEATH
Russell Scott Brinegar

My name is Russell Scott Brinegar. I, like so many others in this scientific age, lived the first 54 years of my life under the predominant scientific paradigm, that the material world is all there is, that the so-called paranormal is the domain of charlatans and wishful thinkers, that consciousness is simply an epiphenomenon of the physical brain, and that when we die we are simply gone into an eternity of unconsciousness.

However, on August 18, 2009, that paradigm was shattered by a personal near-death experience that provided me with an unexpected "snapshot" of the interdimensional underpinnings of the physical universe. Prior to this date, I had relegated reports of near-death experiences to the category of chemicals released into the brain as a person approaches physical death, and that these chemicals often produce experiences that seem real to the person dying, but are actually just a bizarre coping mechanism that nature developed over time via the process of evolution.

That is, until it happened to me. During this near-death experience, as I was dying from a heart attack, something happened to me that I would later come to understand through an investigation into ufology as the "Oz Factor." Time stood still and all noises stopped as I realized I was about to discover if my life-long perception of death was correct. Instead of descending into the blackness of unconsciousness, something else entirely occurred. It was as if my approaching death had "googled the universe" and associated links were popping up into my awareness, links that represented individuals I had known in my earthly life, some of whom had passed on already, and, surprisingly, some of whom were still living on earth. Arriving into my immediate presence were a collection of familiar entities that I felt closely associated with, only they were on the other side of the veil now in an etheric, transcendent form.

The most bizarre aspect of this collection of individuals was that *one of them was me*. As I stood there in my yard on a sunny day, having attempted to mow the grass, I was confronted by the inhabitants of another world that I had never believed in, a beautiful transcendent world that included me and a collection of loved ones, in a form that I can only describe as "intelligent lightning" veiled from me in a soft, shadow-like configuration so that the brilliance would not damage my eyes.

I was suddenly standing very close to another inhabited world or dimension beyond the physical realm that I was already a part of and familiar with. Strangely, some of the familiar entities that were now drawing near to me were still living in earthly form with me. What came next was a communication from this world that I can only describe as telepathic or a spiritual download of some sort, an impression, that I now had a choice to make. I knew that I could succumb to the warm invitation to leave the physical world behind at this point in time, or I could choose to live a bit longer in physical form with a new knowledge that reality is an interdimensional continuum, that life really does exist beyond the grave, that there is a whole different world beyond this life that I formerly knew nothing about.

After considering the choice for a few moments, I decided that it would be really cool and interesting to continue to live in physical form with this newly imparted information. I was curious how different life would be now that I knew there was something much more bizarre and complex going on with life than I formerly believed or understood. It was at this point that I realized I needed to get myself to a hospital if I wanted to continue to live.

As I snapped back into the normal awareness of reality that I had always been used to, I walked into the house, retrieved the keys to my car, and drove myself to the hospital. There was no doubt in my mind that I was going to live, because I had just made that choice. I knew that I would be ok no matter what they had to do to address my ongoing heart attack.

When I arrived at the hospital, I pulled up to the front entrance, and walked into the hospital with my keys held out to the person at the information desk. As he came around to greet me, sensing that an emergency was in the works, I asked him calmly if he would mind parking my car for me and bringing me my keys to wherever I was to be taken, and that I was having a heart attack. Another person sat me in a wheelchair and took me to the emergency room, where I was given morphine and informed that I was, in fact, having a heart attack, and that I would have to be driven to Muncie, Indiana by ambulance.

On the way, with the ambulance lights revolving and sirens blaring, I watched the faces of the EMTs as they looked at me, and then up to my worrisome monitor. I remember feeling sorry for them as they thought they were going to lose me during the drive. When we arrived to Ball Hospital in Muncie, doctors were scrubbed up and ready to operate.

They told me that they could either do a bypass operation or try installing stents, but they had to act fast and needed to know what my choice was. I had them quickly give me a rundown of both procedures and elected the less invasive route with the stents, which have now lasted, at the time of this writing in 2017, for 8 years and counting with no problems.

As I was taken from the "cath lab" to my hospital room, I was rolled past Julie, my girlfriend at the time, who had tears running down her face, as they would not let her in to see me because she was not immediate family. This bothered me so much that I made up my mind right then to fix this situation. So, two months later, on October 30, 2009, Julie and I were married, and we are still happily together now. Following this ordeal, I became very interested in everything related to the paranormal. I began researching anything I could get my hands on that could tell me more about what possibly happened to me on the day of my heart attack. I read other people's accounts of their own near-death experiences and found many similarities.

I felt a strong urge to purchase books that I could highlight and make my own. I wanted these books to become a part of me, and absorbed them like a sponge. I investigated all subject matter involving the paranormal. I read about ghosts, poltergeists, fairies, ancient aliens, UFOs, the Djinn, cryptids, entity encounters, anything and everything having to do with the underlying interdimensional nature of reality, to compare these phenomena with my own experience.

I began collecting so many books on the subject that I was constantly purchasing new bookshelves to put them in. I was on a new adventure with a new understanding, and was having a lot of fun reading the vast amount of UFO material that exists in the public domain.

I discovered authors like computer scientist and ufologist Jacques Vallee, investigative journalist John Keel, French mathematician Aime Michel, zoologist Ivan T.

Sanderson, and so many others. I examined all of the developing interpretations of the UFO phenomenon, such as the Extraterrestrial Hypothesis, the Interdimensional Hypothesis, the Geophysical Hypothesis, intelligent plasmas, Jungian interpretations, and various versions of the Holographic Universe, the Multiverse, String Theory, and the "Simulation Hypothesis" that postulates we are living inside some sort of complex, intentionally-fabricated computer-like Matrix.

Over time, as my volume of notes grew, a bigger picture began to emerge that has something to do with humans being guided, from ancient times, into high technology, culminating in what futurists like Ray Kurzweil are calling the Singularity, predicted to occur sometime between the years 2045-2080. In this spiritual and technological journey, there exists an extraterrestrial presence, some of whom are involved with humans for their own benefit at our expense, and others who are genuinely interested in our spiritual welfare.

The way we live our lives and our own personal vibrational resonance determines which faction of cosmic superintelligence we will eventually ally ourselves with. This emerging picture is something that I wanted others to become aware of, so I began turning my personal discoveries and contemplations about UFOs and the paranormal into a readable format that was useful to others.

Finally, in 2016, I published the results of my own personal investigations of and experiences with the paranormal into my book, "Overlords of the Singularity: The Manipulation of Humankind by Hidden UFO Intelligences and the Quest for Transcendence."

A couple of years prior to this I had called Clifford Stone on the telephone and had a great 3 hour conversation with this wonderful man who had been involved with so-called "flying saucer crash retrievals" beginning in the late 1960s. During this conversation, I had mentioned to Clifford that I was working on completing a book about UFOs, so when it was completed, I posted a picture of the cover of the book on Clifford's facebook page, and was soon contacted by Janet and Dr. Sasha Lessin, which led to several live discussions on their radio program.

I have since had the pleasure of meeting and speaking with many interesting experiencers and people who share a common interest in flying saucers, extraterrestrials, and the interdimensional nature of existence. I'm really glad now that I decided back in 2009 to live a while longer in physical form here to share this knowledge and awareness of the otherworldly.

One of the distinct impressions that I received from my near-death experience is that we are here to work on and improve ourselves and our relationships with other people. Some of the people that we are involved with here on earth also have an afterlife involvement with us.

As we live our lives here on Earth, there is already a transcended version of each and every one of us on the other side. Part of our consciousness is invested here while we live here on Earth, while a part of us remains on the other side.

While we are here there is an informational and experiential interaction between the two versions of ourselves, between the temporal and the eternal. It is very important that we use this physical life to learn as much as we can, improve the way we treat other people, and become aware of and correct personal habits and behaviors that bring physical or psychological harm to anyone. Love and knowledge are the keys.

The goal is to live life in a way that is beneficial to the eventual well-being of all parties concerned. This is not an easy thing to do because there are psychological payoffs and neuro-chemical rewards in the brain if we act selfishly. Even conflict itself can be addicting to us. It takes conscious discipline to correct these impulses, but I feel that this is our task on Earth and the reason we are here, to work on ourselves.

The best thing we can do, rather than constantly criticizing what we do not like in others, is correct these things within ourselves and make ourselves an example of what we believe a loving human being should be. Changing ourselves is the most effective way to change the world at large, one person at a time.

In 2016, Russ Brinegar published his book, "Overlords of the Singularity: The Manipulation of Humankind by Hidden UFO Intelligences and the Quest for Transcendence," available from Amazon or Barnes and Noble's websites. The book is available in Kindle version with text-to-speech enabled or in printed version (545 pages) with excellent cover art.

Russell Scott Brinegar ~ Bio

Russ Brinegar was born in Fort Wayne, Indiana on September 12, 1955, and moved with his mother and father to Titusville, Florida in 1956, where Russ spent his childhood on the "Space Coast." As a child, he was very interested in science fiction, and collected 1962 *Mars Attacks* bubble gum cards. He and his father enjoyed the very first episode of the original "Star Trek" together on television.

Russ was raised as a fundamentalist Christian, but began questioning the stories in the Bible at around the age of 13, an inquiry that followed him into adulthood. As a teenager, Russ enjoyed watching the Apollo Saturn 5 moon rockets launch from Cape Kennedy, Florida.

At the age of 17 Russ entered the US Army as a gunner on an 81 mm mortar crew. While he was in the Army, his family moved back to Bloomington, Indiana, so that is where he moved to live following his discharge from the Army. Russ attended Indiana University in Bloomington, Indiana as a theater major prior to embarking on a career in sales that lasted about 15 years.

At the age of 37, he re-entered college, attending both Indiana University at Bloomington, and IUPUI in Indianapolis for a Bachelor's Degree in Occupational Therapy. At the age of 45, Russ published his first book, *"Outgrowing the Bible: The Journey from Fundamentalism to Freethinking,"* which is still available on Amazon. At the time Russ wrote this first book, which explores the origins and content of the Bible from a scientific perspective, he considered himself an agnostic, a scientific material reductionist who believed that, when humans die, they are simply gone forever in unconsciousness.

Nine years later, at the age of 54, Russ experienced a heart attack and NDE (near-death experience) that revealed the underlying interdimensional nature of reality. This experience completely changed the paradigm by which Russ had always lived his life. Inspired by his NDE, Russ embarked on a personal journey into the so-called "paranormal" for several years, researching subjects such as: ghosts; poltergeists; cryptids; The Djinn; elementals; UFOs; and extraterrestrial or interdimensional entity encounters. He began keeping a notebook of information and ideas, which he eventually honed into a readable manuscript.

In 2016, Russ published his latest book, *Overlords of the Singularity: The Manipulation of Humankind by Hidden UFO Intelligences and the Quest for Transcendence.* His book is available in digital format for Kindle devices on Amazon, with text-to-speech enabled, and also in printed format (545 pages) on both Amazon and Barnes and Noble websites. This book contains much food for thought for both UFO skeptics and believers, and covers a wide range of topics from ancient UFO sightings, so-called "flying saucer crashes" and recovered technology, the history of UFO cults, trace evidence cases, and the alien agenda, which Russ believes has something to do with the impending technological Singularity, predicted by futurists like Ray Kurzweil to occur sometime between the years 2045-2080.

As author William Bramley indicated in "The Gods of Eden," Earth appears to have an extraterrestrial presence, one faction of which is using humanity for their own ends, and another faction who take a genuine interest in human development and spirituality. In this book, Russ shares the intimate details of his near-death experience in 2009, and explores the relationship between UFOs and such topics as the "Simulation Hypothesis," Transhumanism, and the coming Singularity. With this book, Mr. Brinegar hopes to remove at least one more layer from Earth's haunting flying saucer mystery, the inner nature of reality itself, and gain a better understanding of the ultimate destiny of humankind. His book can be ordered from Amazon.com, BarnesandNoble.com, or Createspace.com.

Russ Brinegar was born on September 12, 1955 in Fort Wayne, Indiana. When he was one year old, his family moved to Titusville, Florida, where he grew up on the Space Coast. He graduated from Titusville High School in 1973 and joined the US Army as a gunner on an 81 mm mortar crew for the 101st Airborne Infantry. When he was in the Army, his family moved from Titusville, Florida, to Bloomington, Indiana, where his father was originally from.

When he was discharged from the Army he went to school at Indiana University as a theater major. He left school to embark on a sales career for the next decade and a half. Then, at the age of 37, he re-entered college at IU in Bloomington and IUPUI, earning a Bachelor's Degree in Occupational Therapy. Following graduation at the age of 42, Russ has worked in the geriatric field of therapy. Russ was raised as a fundamentalist Christian in the Baptist denomination, but began questioning the stories in the Bible at around the age of 13. Russ lived most of his adult life as an agnostic, and very scientifically oriented.

In 2000, Russ wrote his first book, "Outgrowing the Bible: The Journey from Fundamentalism to Freethinking, which is still on Amazon.

On August 18, 2009, Russ was mowing his lawn during lunch break from work when he had a heart attack and nearly died. During this near death experience (NDE), the underlying interdimensional nature of reality was revealed to Russ and he was given a choice to cross over to the other side, or remain on Earth by a small gathering of transcendent entities, once of which was a transcended version of him.

This experience most closely matches David Chalmers "Mind-Body Matrix" version of the Simulation Hypothesis, in which a "higher self" that exists outside of time invests a portion of its consciousness into earthly form, and there is a continuous informational exchange of information between the temporary earthly life and the transcendent eternal life.

Following his NDE, Russ became very interested in UFOs and the paranormal, and began a journey of personal research that lasted many years. He noticed that just about all the authors in the UFO field spent most of their time on ascertaining the reality of flying saucers and ufonauts, but were unable to piece together any patterns as to the actual alien agenda at hand.

Russ kept a notebook of his research, and notices a pattern in the UFO encounters and communications that appeared to be leading Humankind on a path of ever-increasing technology. Russ concluded that UFOs have something to do with the impending technological Singularity, predicted by futurists like Ray Kurzweil to occur sometime between the years 2045-2080.

EXPERIENCES OF A WALK-IN FROM BOÖTES ANDROMEDA GALAXY

Hildegard Gmeiner

THE ESCALATOR

The first time I had an encounter in the 'light' I was in Siegburg/Germany. In the spring of 1992 I had taken my 11-months-old baby, Dominik, to my parents' home in Germany, which is in a small village 30 minutes east of Bonn, not far from the river Rhein.

I had left the baby at home with mother and had taken her car to town to run some errands for her and to look for some presents for my two older boys to take home with me to Canada the following Monday. I remember standing on the escalator holding on to the handrail. Then suddenly, as if someone was closing a black curtain on a massive stage, I saw black draping showing up in the left corner of my left eye as well as from the right corner of my right eye, limiting my peripheral vision until suddenly everything turned black, as if someone had suddenly switch off a light.

The very same instant the darkness vanished and I suddenly found myself surrounded by magnificent bright, iridescent light. It was so bright in fact that I wanted to cover my eyes with my hands. Much to my surprise, I suddenly realize I had neither hands, nor a body and yet I was fully aware. I was able to think and somehow I was fully conscious. I had an inner dialog going on, much the same way I had been used to while being in my physical body.

How could it be that I could think, see, feel and hear, even without my body?

The first thought which came to mind was, I am finally dead. I was thinking that my body had finally given up. Ever since the birth of my third child I had been losing excessive amounts of weight, quite unintended and my body had become very weak, almost too weak to cope with the demands of taking care of the daily routine of a stay-at-home mother of three little children. For months I had been seeing different medical specialist in hopes the cause for my steadily deteriorating health could be found, yet to no avail.

I just had been losing too much weight, too quickly so I though. Maybe I had been too skinny, too weak to handle my life and I had died. Though this thought initially gave me a sense of relief, considering the stress of having spent most of last year, going from one medical specialist's office to another, in an attempt to find out what was wrong with my body, I was overcome by fear and felt very much confused, as to what had happened to me.

A sudden panic overcame me. What would happen to my three beautiful children, if, in fact, I had just died? Who would look after them and care for them, with me being dead and with their father always being away from home for his work; traveling a great deal, locally and internationally?

Suddenly my inner panic attack was interrupted by a very

clear and loving voice. It seemed to come from the far distance, almost right out of the center point of the light source which appeared to be miles away, yet I could hear the voice as clearly as if the speaker were standing next to me. Even though I cannot exactly recall what was said verbatim, I can still recall the way this voice made me feel. I felt at home, as if after a very long and hard time away, I had finally had come back home.

Before this happened, I lived a seemingly perfect life with a husband and three little boys in the suburbs of Toronto. I had been able to care for my family, until in the summer of 1991 my physical health seemed to have taken a turn for the worse. After what felt like a very long time of never belonging and fitting in anywhere, in spite of outer appearances, I had a sense that I belonged somewhere, I belonged here into this space where I was at this very moment.

This feeling was very strong, like I had never before experienced. The words spoken from the voice in the distance drew me closer. Even though I don't remember the exact words, again the feeling they created inside of me was overwhelmingly powerful. Never before had I experienced anything like this before. I could identify with what was said and longed to be like the person who was speaking.

Even though I had not been able to make out any of the shapes or forms I had been used to while living in my body, as a drew closer to the light source, it took on sparkly rainbow colors, much like the fiery explosion of color a beautiful opal might bring about, when hit by sunlight.

It was most fascinating how my just thinking about wanting to explore the source point of that incredible light, had me be there in the very same instant, I had been thinking about it.

While much of my inner monolog was going on, the voice was speaking to me. The sounds the voice made were comparable to those of a middle-aged male voice. It felt as if I was standing there listening to this formless something, which was explaining something, I very much agreed with. Yet, I have no verbatim recall of what was actually said.

I longed for the day when I would be able to speak with such clarity, inner conviction and confidence. Inside me was this deep desire to take a stand, make my view points and opinions known and be able to completely live and stand up for my innermost convictions.

All of the above, I recalled, was totally opposing the way I had been living in my body, here on Earth for thirty-three years. The life I had been leading, before seemingly snapping out of the body and having come to this luminous place, had been one of doing what I believed others wanted me to do.

I didn't realize until many years later that I unconsciously had been living according to the values, beliefs and priorities of others. I had been too shy, too insecure and had had too little self-confidence to stand up for my beliefs, needs and desires. In fact, in those days, I was even unaware that I had a right to have my needs met in the first place, just like any other person on the planet.

Unconsciously, I had created a life of quiet desperation,

sleeplessness, sicknesses, and stress. I had become a notorious pleaser, who was driven by the fear emotion of guilt, shame, blame, judgement, most powerful judgement of me. I was stuck in the self-perception of been a victim and my habitual negative thought patterns, which had me never be good enough, no matter what I did, had been pushing me to the brim of unconscious self-destruction.

Little did I know in those days, that illness is the last ditch effort on part of our soul attempting to get our attention, because I had continuously refused to listen to its subtler messages.

As mentioned before, no sooner had I thought of wanting to go to the source of the point of light in the distance, I was already there.

As I was approaching the light, and the rainbow colors begun to surround me, there was a very soft and gentle feeling of something much more powerful and profound than receiving a hug here on Earth. I felt a sudden embrace and yet it was not just a hug. It was as super soft and gentle, as if someone was wrapping me in the most expensive, thick and fluffy Cashmere blanket. Maybe a newborn baby feels that way, when her/his mother wraps her/him in a warm blanket, and loving holds her baby in her arms.

The voice said this was my true home, the source from where my journey to Earth had started. I was told while I was very welcome there; the time to stay there had not yet come.

"You have to complete your missions," a voice had said

very lovingly.

I had still commitments to fulfill other places, and therefore, I was to go back, to complete what I had begun. Once the whole mission was going to be completed, I would be welcome to come back here into the light.

Surprisingly I didn't feel the least bit rejected by the statement, nor by yet another super soft and gentle farewell hug. Much to the contrary, it was a very gentle, almost feather light embrace I felt before I seemingly was snapped back into a completely different world once again, back into my physical body.

Within the next moment I was awakened by the smell of coffee. A middle aged lady, I had never seen before, had brought a cup to the desk next to the stretcher bed I was lying on and encouraged me to drink the coffee she had brought for me. She told me that I had fainted on the store escalator, cut my legs a bit, which she was going to attend to shortly, yet thank goodness, no other harm had been done, as she put it.

She told me I was in C & A department store in Siegburg, in their first aid room. Her supervisor had been in touch with the local EMS services and they were going to come and attend to me shortly.

My body was cold, my heart was racing and my mind was working overtime, for I wanted to figure out what really happened and what had brought on this fainting spell.

The emergency service did arrive, ran some tests and

gave me a clean bill of health. My caregiver was instructed to make sure I would drink more of the stiff, black, strong-smelling coffee. Then I was to be sent on my way on foot through the pedestrian area to the local hospital for a further check-up, just to be on the safe side.

I drank the coffee, which made my heart pounding even stronger and I felt as if my whole body was getting an electrical jolt, as if I had just touched a massive power line. All I could think of is water. I need to have lots of water to drink and rest some more, I thought. After about another hour of resting and filling up on water in the first aid room of said department store, I ever so slowly made my way to the hospital.

It was one of the first warm spring mornings in April. The sun was already warm enough for the café house chairs to be filling up with sun worshippers and the birds were out looking to benefit from some crumbs of the early lunch and coffee time crowd.

I managed to find a spot on one of the park benches in the Siegburg market square, allowing the sun to kiss my face for a while. It didn't take long before a lady sat down beside me and started to chitchat. I did my best to make polite conversation, yet I couldn't be very engaged for my thoughts were back home in Canada, with my two older boys, who were being looked after for the week, by a family friend during the day, while their dad was a work. This had been the very first time I had been away from them for one week, which added another load to my already tumultuous inner world.

My thoughts travelled back in time and distance and

conversations with other mothers came to mind, who had suggested, I was to hire help, so I could take two days a week of from parenting and the housework, which, of course, would never end. I had never thought about it that all workers/employees get two days a week off from gainful employment tasks. However, a mother always has to be on-call 24/7 365 days a year, without a break. The wear and tear of this was clearly showing up in my bad bill of health, my nervousness, thinness and lack of sleep and rest had been clearly eroding away at my overall health, like roaring ocean waves carving holes into a mountain side.

Once I had made the decision to give my body a regular day off, during which I focused all my attention on self-rejuvenation, my body did fall apart even more. Once I was free up for a day or two of the daily schedule, my body really felt exhausted. I became aware of how overstretch my system was, once I attempted to give it a break.

Many of my days off, I spent sitting by the lake doing nothing. I usually took a journal book or a book to read and sat on a park bench doing nothing. Yet this had me be even more exhausted, than before. Sometimes I would go to see a Shiatsu Therapist or a Chiropractor, for my shoulders had been in knots for a very long time, and my lower back pain had been equally permanent, ever since I had had children.

Sometimes I would go to an exercise class at Holy crest Public School, or I went for a swim at the near-by Olympian sports complex in Centennial Park.

Needless to say, the first little while my mind was driving my almost crazy. My inner negative mind chatter was telling me how irresponsible and selfish I was being, wasting my time sitting by the water's edge doing nothing and paying a babysitter for looking after my children.

Add to that many of my husband's negative comments would come to mind, and play them out over and over again, like a broken record. He was of the opinion that my need for time to myself was truly exaggerated, since in his opinion I had always plenty of time to myself, whenever the kids were sleeping. Sadly, he did get that for close to six years straight; I never ever had one full night of uninterrupted sleep. It seemed to me that societal norms appeared to considering a stay-at-home's 24/7 on-call work schedule, not worthy of the same respect and consideration for rest, as that of a woman, who was gainfully employed outside the home.

I had been the one nursing, while my spouse had been sleeping and over time I felt like a squished out prune, while my four men being the four kings of the castle, commanding me, their willing servant, about. Not surprising then, my body had been running on empty. -

The early spring sun felt ever so very good on my face, as I was sitting there in the City of Siegburg market square that day in Germany. I was waiting for my energies to grow stronger, so I could continue my walk to the Ring Strasse, where the Kreiskrankenhaus / Siegburg Hospital, was located.

While I had been with my thoughts in Canada, the lady

who sat next to me on the park bench in Siegburg/Germany wanted to know whether I was alright. I told her my story of having collapsed on the department store escalator and that I was on my way to the near-by hospital for another check-up.

"No worries," she said calmly.

"They will be unable to find what's wrong with you," she continued, "for what's right with you, they consider wrong, because they really don't understand the bigger picture now, do they?" she said in a very stern voice.

The lady must have been in her mid-sixties. She was very elegantly dressed. Her brown hair was tied into a bun, showing from underneath her elegant, light woolen, spring hat. Her hands were protected by fine leather gloves, which complemented the light color in her brown-patterned, spring coat, and equally matched the little purse hanging of her left arm, as well as her cream-colored, low-heeled dress-shoes.

Who was this woman? There had been so many vacant benches near-by she could have chosen to sit on and yet, she decided to sit right next to me. I didn't mind it; however, it made me think, nonetheless.

"You know, dear," the lady spoke again, "there are things between Heaven and Earth no one really understands. Do you believe in angels or the paranormal in general?"

The lady curiously looked at me, seemingly waiting for my response. I could feel her eyes staring at me even though my eyes were closed and I was pretending to not have heard her question. It was ever so weird, hearing her talk about angels, the paranormal and stuff between Heaven and Earth, just now, after I had been in this place of inexplicable brightness and light, just minutes before.

"I am not sure," I heard myself respond to her. I opened my eyes and turned slightly to look at her.

"After my interesting fainting experience, on the C&A escalator earlier today, I am not sure what to believe anymore. But, heaven knows, I could use a crowd of angels supporting me right now, after all that has been shaking down in my life lately."

I sat still, without even turning or looking at her. I was hoping she would finally leave and be on her way, leaving me with my thoughts. It might have been about five minutes later, when I asked her, what specifically had her asked me this question about angels, yet there was no answer. The lady was gone, but I hadn't felt her getting up from the wooden bench, nor had I heard her footsteps; I had not notice her leaving.

I wasn't sure what to make of this strange encounter. I decided to continue on to the hospital and then return home to my mother's house as soon as the hospital staff would give me the all clear.

Alone on the bench, I fell back into my pondering about what previously had happened in my life before I had traveled to Germany with Baby Dominik for a week's visit at my parent's farm.

AIRPORT ROAD PARKING LOT

It was a Friday around 11 o'clock in the morning. My van was parked in a parking lot and I had just put the baby, my four-year-old and my six-year-old in their respective car seats. Our six-months-old Golden Retriever Puppy was in the back.

Upon closing the sliding door on the passenger side and while walking around the front of my van I notice how the sun, my parked car was south at that time, was becoming incredibly bright. It struck me as very unusual.

Once I was sitting in the driver seat, I started the engine and the radio come on, saying something which caught me instant interest, so I sat for a second to listen before putting the car in gear and leaving the parking lot.

There I sat with the car engine running, now ignoring the sounds of the radio, and even more transfixed on the sun, which now appeared to be growing in size and even in brilliance and brightness. Is that at all possible, I remember thinking.

The next thing I knew; I awoke in the driver seat of my car. The engine was no longer running, even though the key was still in the "Drive" position. All three boys were fast asleep in their car seats, as was the puppy dog in the back of the van. – I was stunned. I could not remember a day or a night, when all the three boys had been sleeping at the same time.

What had just happened here?

I found my car seat in a reclining position, I was wearing

my seatbelt, the car doors, which I usually would never look from the inside, now were locked and it seemed that more than an hour had gone by, since I had first put the children in their car seats.

Since during those days, I was very much plagued with self-doubt, partly due to the fact that the medical experts still had not been able to come up with answers, as to what the cause of my ongoing and irregular fainting spells were, I did my best to ignore what had happened and did my best to pretend it never happened.

I had been reprimanded, criticized and belittled one too many a time by people who claimed to know more about my body and my whole being than, me, the only person, truly having the experiences, that I decided to ignore the whole incident.

BIGHAM CRESCENT

Ever since the first time I fainted in Germany, strange things happened in my life. I would switch on the radio or the television at home, and what was said appeared to be just meant for me. It was as if somehow, someone was communicating with me, however, not in the usual way, human beings would communicate with each other.

For instance, I might be seeing a newspaper advertisement, or a truck would drive by me on the road and the advertisement or the company name would hit me in a very unusual and almost verbally indiscernible manner.

I had situations during which I had poured myself a hot cup of coffee I had just brewed, during the early afternoon, at home in my kitchen. The two older boys were in Kindergarten and at school, the baby had been sleeping. However, when I wanted to sit down and drink the coffee, it was as cold as if it had come straight out of the refrigerator and the baby was crying in the crib upstairs.

Obviously, a great deal of time passed and yet I could not remember what had happened and where I had been. Judging by my kitchen clock and the fact that the little one usually had his afternoon nap between 1 – 3:00 PM, I noticed I was missing about two hours.

Considering that when these events begun to happen 25 years ago, I had no understanding, nor any explanation for what was happening, I trusted the opinions of people around me more than my inner knowing and understanding. In those days even though I had grown up on a farm in Germany, was able to speak three languages and successfully worked in international trade d in the fields of translations and interpreting, I viewed myself as an ordinary, not very educated women.

I had been already criticized many times and many different people, for having too vivid an imagination, I chalked this event up yet again, to my overstretched nervous systems, which might have been playing tricks on me yet again.

However, in the summer of 1992 something happened, which was to upset and rearrange my life in a very profound way, and it made the beliefs I had once been holding, as the life I had once been living for 33 years, fall apart like a house of cards, seemingly overnight.

DOMINIK

"Dominik, stop," I heard myself yell as I ran after the little one headed straight for the road.

Suddenly the familiar black velvet theatre curtains appeared yet again in the left corner of my left eye, as well as the very right corner of my right eye.

The next moment I was finding my white-colored body lying on a table, surrounded by four humanoid-shaped people to my right, as well as to my left. Two people were standing by my feet and two by my head.

Interestingly enough I was not afraid of them, much to the contrary. I felt happy, light and even joyous to see them all. I was feeling very safe there in this space, which seemed to be very bright. I can only assume that I was in a room, for I couldn't make out walls in the sense that I had been used to from my life on Earth.

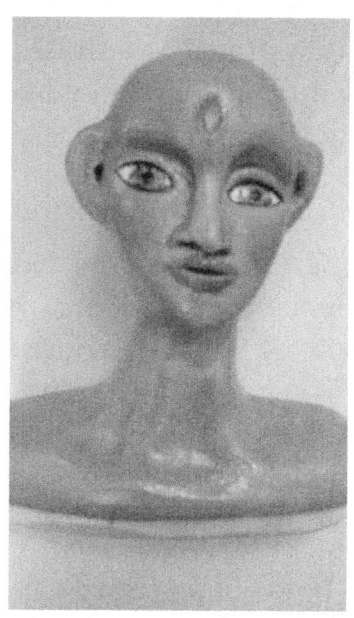

The person standing closest to my right I saw best. It felt as if he was a man. He had beautiful almond-shaped eyes, with a dark-blue iris, which seemed to be surrounded by a super-white. His skin was like that of a like golden-bronzy tanned, silvery/blond haired northern European person.

The skin was as pure and wrinkle-free like that of a thirty-year-old Earth human, or possibly even better described as the pureness of that of a newborn baby.

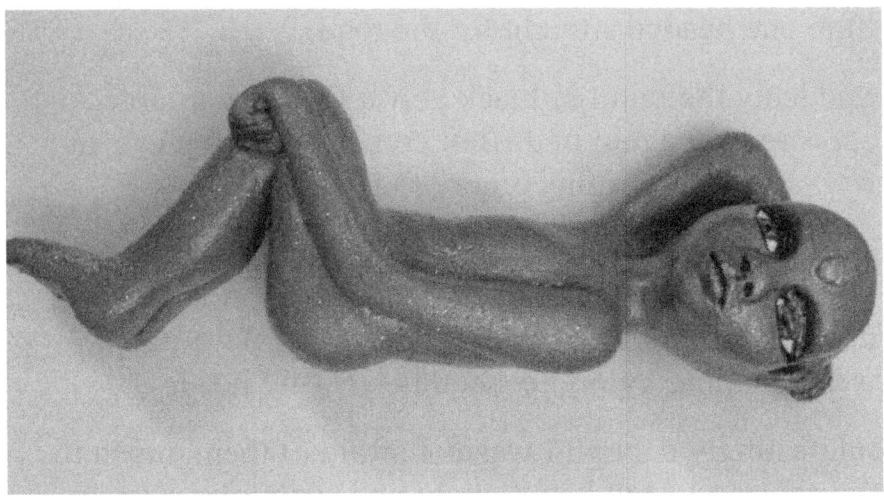

All twelve people looked very much the same. They had straight, chest-long hair, which was whitish-silvery, platinum in color. They were all dressed the same in what appeared to be white overalls.

The person closest to my right was telepathically telling me, I had volunteered to be a "Walk-In" and hence I was going to be experience regular energetic upgrades like this one, from time to time. My 3-D body had been animated by another aspect of my essence-soul self, who only wanted thirty-three years of experience in a physical embodiment in the Earthly realm. Hence an agreement was made, that yet another soul aspect of the same source energy, was going to take over this 3-D body, for it to be animated by a seventh-dimensional consciousness, which would bring with it the qualities of a consciousness-scientist from Boötes/Andromeda Galaxy.

I was not to worry, all was going to be well, and I was

going to be brought onto Andromedan ships from time to time, for check-ups and upgrades, as it was going to be deemed necessary over time.

Before I had become aware of that space, in which I was surrounded by the 12 Andromedans, I had in a split-second, seen the neighbors on Bigham Crescent coming together on the sidewalk.

A lady in a pink dress suit was holding little Dominik, my eldest son Florian, was holding the hand of his toddler brother, Timotheus. His face was showing complete fright and fear. Next door neighbors' grandparents had been out gardening and apparently had alarmed other neighbors to come and help carry my body, which had been lying motionless on the sidewalk into the house at 75 Bigham Crescent, were we lived at that time.

I remember seeing an ambulance and saw my body being carried on a stretcher and put in the ambulance while the onlookers stood their motionless. They resembled ice-sculptures in the deep of winter. The face of my eldest son froze into my memory forever.

Once awake in the emergency room at Etobicoke General Hospital, the health care professionals couldn't tell me anything else, but that all my vital signs were fine. The cause of what had my body collapse out of the blue that sunny summer afternoon in the west end of Toronto could not be established.

INTEGRATION CHALLENGES

When the emergency room doctor asked me, what had

happened, I described to him, exactly what I have been sharing above. I told him, that my 7-D essence energy had been swopping places with the previous 3-D essence energy aspect of the same soul aspect, or something like that.

He listened to me for a short while and then immediately instructed the nurse to get some medication to calm down my nervous system, since it was apparently clear to him that I had been experienced some sort of a nervous breakdown.

I refused to be given a needle and requested to be given pills instead, which I then could administer at my discretion. I was suddenly overcome by panic and fear, fear about the hospital not being a safe place for me and that the people there, who were there to help me, could actually harm me.

The man sitting next to my gurney was apparently my next-of-kin, my husband of ten years. I remember him saying, how inconvenient it was, for him to always be called out of very important business meetings by phone calls from the emergency department of the local hospital. I ought to get it together somehow and I should get on with life.

I looked at that person, and couldn't believe I was apparently married to this man, even though the words husband, nor marriage painted a clear picture in my mind either. He had told me that I was his wife and we had three small children together.

All of this was very weird to me, for it was as if I had never been in that hospital or with the person before, even though, as I was to learn and remember later on, two of our children had actually been born in that very hospital.

In the car on the way back to our home, it felt as if I was sitting in a theater watching a very weird movie, about someone else's life. The cars rushing by the passenger side window frightened me, as did the fact that there were so many cars racing past each other in such close approximation.

Everything around me felt foreign and new to me, including the clothes on my back.

Inside my head I was panicking, screaming for someone to please get me out of there. What crazy place had I been dumped in? How could it be that I had been abandoned by my people? Yet I couldn't even remember who my people were.

What I could remember and what I was able to hear from inside of myself was the calming voice, the very same one I had heard a year and a half before, when I had been in the light, after the escalator incident in the German department store that happened.

The voice said:

"All is well, you are not alone, we are going to coach you through this transition and we will help you integrate the new energies. You will not want for anything; even though you might not get everything you want."

I was furious. What the hell was going on? What did this all mean? Couldn't someone, just get me out of there?

Once the car stopped outside a subdivision home, where almost every house was looking the same as the one next door, and had one or two cars, parked outside a single car-garage, and the door to one of them open, three little children run towards me yelling:

"Mummy, Mummy, you are home!!!"

I was choked and scared at the same time, for I initially had no recollection of who these children were. Nor did I remember anything about the house; we apparently had been living in at that point, for over seven years.

Then the children asked, "Mummy, what's for dinner?" I didn't know what to say. In fact my inner fear and panic grew even more intense.

I remember speaking to the voice in my head, which at this point came back with the following answer, "I got you help to deal with this, my beloved. Please meet, Ashtar-Athena. She will guide you through all you will have to know about what it means to be a woman, a mother, and a wife in this world."

From that moment on I heard a female voice, explaining me everything to do with and related to looking after the three little ones, as well as about everything a woman in that situation and lifestyle had do know. The male voice would come in every now and then and give me some background information, he felt I needed to have or to guide me in a direction of where, I would find useful information or meet people, who could help me gain new understanding, as to how to heal and meant the very run-down body I was seemingly stuck in.

However, the more, I was attempting to explain to my husband what had happened to me, and about my experiences in the light, the special messages from radio and television and advertisements, the missing time and having seen the 12 Andromedans with Platinum long, straight hair, the more convinced he became that I was mentally ill. This ultimately led to, what I like to call, my great escape in February 1994.

Once again LuiMar's, the Andromedan's voice had guided me to pack up the kids and the dog and escape from that subdivision house, as long as still at liberty to do so. Details about this escape can be found in one the chapters of my upcoming book, in which I am describing my whole life story, beginning with the walk-in experience described herein.

HOUSE FIRE

It was the 23rd December 2014. My blended family, I was in a new relationship and had a 10-year-old daughter with my common-law partner, a wonderful step-father to my three sons from my marriage. We had been living a log home, in Northumberland County in Eastern Ontario.

LuiMar, my Andromedan Walk-In support partner, had been telepathically guiding my every step for over a decade at that time, and I had just finished writing the first draft of a 250-page manuscript about my walk-in experience and my spiritual life journey. Again, upon LuiMar's telepathic prompting I had gone back to college to study broadcast journalism, even though, a part of me had no intention to ever be working in that field. However, I had learned over the years to trust in my inner wisdom, and the telepathic guidance, which had brought me this far.

Colleges, Universities and schools were closed for Christmas break and it had been the first full day I had been able spend at home, attending to the preparations for Christmas. We had put the Christmas tree up the Sunday before and every day, more and more beautifully wrapped parcels appeared underneath the tree.

The flames of the fire in the wood stove had been giving the logs of our living room, a very special and festive glow that very evening, before we went to bed, as did the electric Christmas lights on the beautifully decorated tree. It felt so good for change to feel on top of the tasks at hand for a change and to be ready for the holiday celebrations to begin.

That night I remember going to bed with a sense of accomplishment, joy and contentment I had not been feeling over the past months, during which there never seemed to have enough to do anything.

Then at 3:00 am in the morning, I woke up, put on my Birkenstock sandals and run downstairs. All the lights in the house were on. Once in the kitchen I was met with a loud voice from the basement to stay upstairs and to call the fire department, since there apparently was a fire on the far side of the basement.

The phone lines were dead. I yelled back to my partner who was still in the basement, trying to put the fire out with water from the laundry room tap that he would have to get his cell phone to call 911, for in those days, we only had one cell phone in the house.

I could now smell the fire in the basement. I run upstairs yelling for our daughter and her friend Erica to get up and please go and wait for me on the deck outside the front door. Erica had been at our house for a long-awaited sleepover. Thankfully she had been already on her way down the stairs, with our daughter Meriya in tow.

I ordered them step onto the deck and to wait outside, while I was going to run to the master bedroom to grab my purse, which had the car keys in it, so I could drive to Erica home, and to have the children sheltered there, seeing that none of our out-buildings were heated. It was also instantly clear to me that once the fire trucks came rolling down the long, narrow driveway of our rural, forested property; I was not going to be able to get out with my van to drive Erica home.

The girls went out onto the deck, while I run upstairs, yelling down to my partner to please get out of the basement and stay with the girls until I was going to be back downstairs with my car keys.

I hurried down the stairs purse, blankets and clothes in hand and thought to myself, well that worked out well, when suddenly, it all went black in front of my eyes again, just like I had experienced so many times before.

There I was yet, again, in the space of iridescent brilliant light. I couldn't make out any shapes, or forms. This time, I didn't see the people with the long-platinum colored hair with their Almond-shape beautiful dark-blue eyes, all I was aware of, was the soft touch of an invisible hand and a voice, which was ever so calm and familiar.

It was gently was communicating with me.

Time appeared to be standing still and enjoyed being in the space I was in and I had no recollection of anything related to the house fire. Yet again, the voice was speaking to me and I found myself agreeing and feeling very happy about the encounter and about what I had learned during this time.

My hand was feeling this gentle soft touch all the while until I felt a very gently push from behind me, as if someone was pushing me forward from behind, yet without any force. I was told to walk straight forward and out the front door, where it would be safe, yet all I could see was white light, not my front door.

Suddenly, as if awakening from a long and restful sleep, I heard a voice calling me from afar.

"Mum, it is freezing cold out here…come out now…you must open the car for us now…are you coming?"

I felt my hand touching what felt like the window, which was a part of our front entrance door. I soon found the door handle, which was still of normal temperature, I open the door and I was greeted by two shivering girls, whose survival depended on me getting them into a warm place immediately.

I instantly became aware of my surroundings again, in full consciousness, once my feet stepped out of the house, into knee-high snow and my face was hit by ice-rain.

Thankfully everyone survived the fire.

These are just a few sampling so events which I have experienced over the last 25 years, which cannot be explained, nor understood easily by trying to force them within the constraints and the limited frames of reference of commonly excepted, old paradigms. I would like to invite the reader of these stories, to open their hearts and minds to the possibility that humanity is part of a greater whole.

We are part of intelligence, which is not limited to time and space. Nor is it limited to what our logical condition mind believes possible. It's already commonly understand that that our five physical senses fool us all the time and at the same time, there is no official information, nor education, as to how a human is to utilize their extra-sensory perceptions and abilities.

Though there are undoubtedly those who know more about the universe and it's workings that are made public knowledge.

Furthermore, I might just be, that access to more of who we are is very much an individual, soul-specific journey, for which general rules, the way rules are understood by our species right now, don't apply.

As a result of my now over two-decades long research and quest to find out more about who I am and what, my role is in the universal bigger picture of thing, I am no more convinced than ever that

    a) Intelligent life exists beyond this planet
    b) Human kind has always been guided by off-planet, higher dimensional beings
    c) Extraterrestrial life forms are as real as you and I.

All the stories found in our history books, in religious texts and mythologies have one thing in common, they are describing events, and speak of contacts, which was not commonly understood, nor could they be explained, with which was accepted as common knowledge at that specific time in history.

Which yet brings another question? Is what we have learned from our history books to be blindly trusted or wouldn't it be a better choice to ultimately trust our experiences, our inner wisdom and our unique inner guidance system?

Thank you for your interest in my experiences and for reading this small excerpt. You can contact me via my webpages www.hireawarenss.com or at hildegardgmeiner59@gmail.com

Hildegard Gmeiner ~ Bio

Walk-In, Inspirational Speaker, Intuitive Awareness Consultant, Writer, Poet

Hildegard was born and raised on a farm in Germany. She has a background in languages, international trade, as well as in broadcast journalism and lived in Europe, South Africa and Canada, where she raised her four, now grown, children.

In 1992, when her eldest was only five years old, Hildegard experienced a Source-Essence Exchange. Her Andromedan Soul-Essence-Self traded places with the soul-aspect, which had been animating the physical body up to the age of thirty-three.

She has been receiving ongoing telepathic support and guidance from LuiMar ever since. He is a 7th dimensional consciousness scientist from Boötes/Andromeda Galaxy, tasked with 'Andromedan Walk-In Support'. The "Walk-In Project" deemed necessary by Galactic alliances, in the mid-1940s by virtue of the first nuclear tests being executed by humans on Earth, as well as in space, impacting the greater Galactic community. However, negotiations with Earth government's failed and new ways of shifting the energies on the planet had to be found.

Hildegard's essence had apparently volunteered to be involved in such a mission. The goal was to anchor higher cosmic frequencies on Earth, via telepathic knowledge transfers and expedited DNA-activations through various 'Walk-In' operations. Her sources say, millions of individuals of all walks of life, have been simultaneously contacted, trained and activated worldwide.

Following LuiMar's guidance, Hildegard, not only regained her health, against all medical prognosis, yet she was able to fulfill her responsibilities as a mother of four, in keeping with the mission given by the Andromedans, which was to 'Raise the Children to the Light.' Therefore, Hildegard has deep trust in the wisdom coming to her Andromedan friends.

In 2016 she began to publically speak about her experiences and insights about off-planet intelligences. In her opinion, such contacts between humans and higher-dimensional intelligence have been happening for millennia. However, the truth about that has actively been hidden, preventing humanity to become fully aware of their true Galactic Nature.

She is currently developing her Intuitive Awareness Consulting, Writing and speaking business, designed to assist others on their path of Self-Discovery and Self-Healing. Her objective is to aid people to understand their para-normal experiences.

Her contacts aid her to facilitate the discovery of her client's inner essence voice and wisdom; provide them with tools to consciously live guided by their inner soul-essence self, helping them recognize and overcome unconscious, self-sabotaging choice mechanisms and self-destructive behavior patterns.

Hildegard has a children's book to be published, and is currently working on a book about her personal spiritual journey, and a text about the cosmic significance of the Divine Feminine during this Aquarian era.

You can reach out to her via her website: www.hireawareness.com

hidlegard@hireawareness.com

COVERT ABDUCTION: AUTOBIOGRAPHY OF MIND CONTROL
Miesha Johnston

I write this book to let you know, no matter what you have gone through in your life. You can change your life to a positive happy experience. To what I call Love & Light. I want to help others who have gone through similar things. To let them know that they are not alone, not crazy and they don't have to be victims. I started my groups in 1992 to provide a safe place for others to share their experiences rather they are positive, which most are concerning the ETs or the negative experiences, which are such things as I am writing about, that happened to me.

I believe that most of my ET experiences have been of a positive and spiritual nature. I will write about some of the positive and some of the negative things that have happened to me in my life but I am not a victim or the result of these things that happened to me. I am who I am because of the things that I have experienced in my life, rather they were good or bad. They made me a more discerning, non-judgmental, understanding and loving human being which is very necessary for the groups I facilitate and the people I counsel.

I have been aware of the Elite & military involvement in my own contact off and on throughout most of my life. I do not know who exactly these groups are and who has abducted me but I believe it to be a small faction within our military and shadow government.

I have had several abductions where I started out with an alien only to end up into the hands of the military. Or be dropped off by the ETs and be picked up by the military, on the same night or a day or two later. I would also wake up in odd places such as in the back of a van, a ranger type jeep or a black helicopter, which the later has caused me to hate flying. I would then be taken to a joint military/alien facility or base. I have memories of going down in elevators to floors where military and aliens seem to be working together.

I have many memories of being taken into a small rooms with gray walls and being interrogated, sometimes treated abusively because I have woke up with bruises all over my body including my arms, inner thighs, ankles, wrist and even my stomach. My interrogators have been men in uniform, people in white smocks and reptilian aliens. (By the way, body scars will show up better under black light that is the same black light as used in night clubs).

My first memory of being taken into DUMB (Deep underground Base) was at age 16 in Arco Idaho in 1965. The last thing I remember I went to bed and the next thing I was with a woman with almost white skin and dark black hair with a widow's peak, she was wearing white. I thought she was a nurse. She handed me over to the tall Reptilians in dark cloaks.

The next memory I have is of being underground and I was part of a sexual project (Told me I was special chose and part of a special race and bloodline and they own me.) It was a horrible ritual I was surrounded by the cloaked ones. I was given drugs that caused extreme sexual arousal a chant was (Abendia) some other names come up. I was wearing a white robe (Priestess). I was raped and sodomized by men and aliens. The reptilians love to suck up my fear adrenalin. They drink up the fear adrenalin. I and other young women/children are laid out on alter with fire all around us. The energy equated with this ritual abuse but aroused me it made me terrified at the same time. It virtually makes you high. I am told that I am a priestess. I chant words, I do not know. My mind goes blank and I lose consciousness. I woke up outside of my house. Was it a horrible dream or perhaps was it a memory from another life? Either way it was a terrifying experience.

We have been led to believe that our day to day life is the only true reality but with your metaphysical teaching you know that is not true. Actually your day to day is the dream. Permission is given on the reality you exist on, all the time.

Much for the childhood is blank, due to severe trauma base mind control perpetrated by my fathers and others. I will go into that memory later on in the book. The next memory I have of such things is when I moved to Pocatello, Idaho and had 8 months of missing time and marriage. But for now I will share more recent experience.

I had one specific memory where I was going down elevator. I saw other people in the elevator. I could see the people on each side of me. Everyone was in a catatonic stage. There was a soldier in front right next to the door with a machine gun. It was kind of funny because there were several people in front of me and some had clothes on, some wore pajamas, some in their underwear and some had no clothes on it all. I think this is due to the different time zones people are taken from.

The elevator stopped and I remember it opened not like a regular elevator a different kind of elevator the doors opened in a zigzag motion. We were shuffled out the door and I was being moved off towards the left and there is kind of a holdup in the people and so the group that was being moved off towards the right where walking ahead of me. I looked at them I saw my 14-year-old son was one of them being taken to a group of tall beige gray aliens. This was so frightening to me, seeing my son taken away and not been able to even move or help him. Knowing what in God's name were they going to do with him? OMG, will I ever see him again?

Men in the black uniforms take me into a small room with a one way glass, The room has grey walls and is about 8 by 8 FT. sized room. I'm sure there is someone watching on the other side. There were 2 that men who escorted me into the room and one who was wearing a lab coat, came in after. I feel it is to administer some kind of a drug. They start yelling at me and using very abusive and profane language. They then started the interrogation and whatever else they do to me. I only have a few memories. I can't remember anything else after that.

Chukatara

I call them these Reps. the Chukatara. I heard this name telepathic. Now I'm not sure if the spelling is right, this is just how it sounded to me. I have since found out that in Africa they call them Chutitari which is quite similar. Could it possibly be the same ones?

One other night I was taken. I was taken to the same small grey room. During this interrogation they were asking me where the bases are. Where is his base where's the alien space craft? I knew they were talking about my dear friend Iyano. I was steadfast in saying I don't know what you're talking about then they'd ask me where the ship is again. I know the ship has landed here where is the ship?

Again I said I have no idea what you're talking about.

I man in a lab coat came in and they forced something down my throat. It was a vile of thick greenish yellow liquid down my throat. It felt like a slime sliding down my throat. It didn't take long for me to understand what it was. I felt it was a drug of some kind because of the way it made me feel. Everything was blurry and moving and I could only see a few feet in any direction. I saw three men in uniforms stood around me. Then a reptilian walked into the room. The reptilian bent down and looked into my eyes. I could not close my eyes as he peered into them. I know that the Reptilian used some type of mind manipulation, like a Vulcan mind melt on me.

He was a dark green about 7 feet tall. I believe it was that's same species that I had seen many times before the underground bases. But this time when he looked into my eyes. I felt like things were being pulled out of my brain it was like he was siphoning my memories out or sifting through them. I had images appear in my head. I would access a picture and then it seemed to be gone and another and another. I felt he was stealing my memories. I thought to myself he's trying to find out about my friends. I can't think about my alien friends and my team. I can't. But, at that moment I heard a very strong loving voice in my head from my friend Iyano saying. "Do not worry you will not give the base location up. I thought to myself oh my God. I can't think of the base I can't think of the base. I tried to think of anything else but that was the only images coming up in my head. I have to think of something else and once again his voice came through do not worry you will not tell our location. To be honest with you I was really gone then from the drugs and I don't remember if he got things out of me or not. I truly have a feeling that he did but perhaps not because I know the implant and the connection I had with Iyano and his group was very strong and very powerful. It may have been strong enough for me not to tell them where the base was. I hoped so because there was a period of time that I did not see Iyano. I was so worried that his base had been compromised.

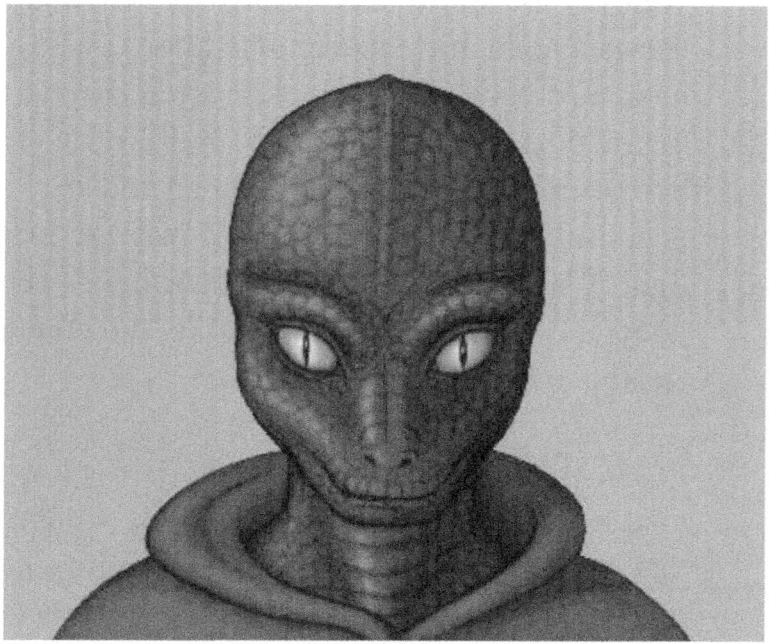

Iyano

I did however see him a few weeks later. He told me that they had to make some adjustments to their base and location. They had evacuated the area by the time the attack came. So thank goodness he made it out. He told me that they know of the reptoid's ways and actions. As they have been at war with them for a Millennia. I want to explain that all communications with Iyano or his team have been through telepathy. When they telepathically communicate with you it is whole thought forms, sentences pictures. At least if works that way for me.

I learned so much from Iyano and the Federation. We truly are spiritual beings living a human life. I learned you can't judge an ET (alien) by how they look. Just because they look scary and maybe ugly to you does not mean they are evil. And Just because they come looking human and are beautiful beings. Does not mean they are from the light. We must be discerning at all time. There is good and bad in all races including the human race. As above so below.

In May of 1999 I was abducted in Sedona while visiting there with my friend, Holley. I went to bed that night but was taken out of my friend's house that we were staying at. I was taken to Boynton Canyon, which is well known in Sedona as a DUMB entrance. They took me in a van with other people they picked up along the way to the canyon. The men who took me wore dark colored uniforms. We were taken inside the mountain, to a laboratory. I was put into coveralls and taken into a hazmat area. Humans in hazmat gear put electrode wires on my head which caused electric impulses to my brain. I remember seeing tall insectoid aliens, I think in the clean room.

While I was gone from my friend's house, they woke up and were looking outside. They decided I must have taken a walk and they went back to bed. The next memory I have is waking up the next morning. They asked me if I had gone on a walk last night. I said, "No I don't think so."

I just remember a very weird dream and I told them about the experience I had in the DUMB. I did have more of an answer to why they took me in the first place reveal itself to me on the way home.

While driving home with three other friends in a car, I was in the passenger side and I receive some kind of a message. I got a psychic impression of a very strange vision of a pod which certainly felt like a reptilian pod. At the same time I was getting a message telepathically from someone who is saying please help us please help us. I got the strong impression it was a hybrid of green color perhaps in the pod.

All of a sudden I started feeling chest pains and thought I was having a heart attack. I had pain in the area of my heart and I was hyperventilating, I couldn't get my breath. I was really worried what was going on. So the driver of the car pulled over, the girls got a pillow and a sleeping bag out of the car. They set it up against the back wheel of the car and I set down. They told me to talk deep breaths but I was still feeling the pain.

Just then, an emergency vehicle pulled up behind the car, where I was seated on the ground. We didn't have time to even make a 911 call, when it pulled up. Two men got out, one wearing white shirt & white pants and one wearing white smocks jacket and camo fatigues pants underneath. He was also wearing military issue black boots. When I saw them I was quite frightened because I knew something didn't feel right. The other girls mentioned that it doesn't look like the normal paramedic truck.

They approached the vehicle but stood about 10 feet away from the car.

I believed it was related to the vision that I had had in the car, just prior to the attack. The two men stated that she looks like she's having a heart attack we need to get her inside and put her on our Defibrillator machine. I told the girls I'm really afraid if I go in that van you'll never see me again.

They brought no EKG, Defibrillator or any other equipment outside of their van. It is my understanding that paramedics and emergency vehicles always have resuscitation and emergency equipment or testing equipment. So for this reason we were sure they were not who they said they were. And I declined to be taken in their truck again. I said I think I'm just having a little heat stroke. I'll be fine.

Right about that time a sheriff's car pulled up on the front of our car. Before the sheriff could exit the vehicle, the two men were back in the van and had left the scene. The pain that I was feeling started lessening and I was feeling better by the time the sheriff walked up to me. He said are you okay everything all right here? I said and my friends backed me up, that I just got a little too much heat and just needed some fresh air. The sheriff said okay that's good. I just wanted to check on you. He got in his car and drove off.

It was very strange thing, the pain stopped right about the time the van pulled out and left us. I felt that they were sending some kind of psychotronic frequency at me. I have been facilitating support groups for people who are MK ultra and targeted individual since 1991. I have had many people talk about how they felt, when they were under attack and having chest pains and a heart attack which was caused by some kind of frequency that was aimed at them. What we found out is that the frequency they shoot at us causes symptoms of a heart attack but it is not a heart attack. But in fact it will worry people so much that they can manifest their own heart attack and it does happen often.

We arrived home on in San Diego at 3:00AM. I was abducted out of my house that morning. Holly was sleeping over to my house she was even sleeping on the floor in the same room I was in, but she again was not taken. I believe she could have been a handler. A handler is a person who is supposed to make sure; I am where they want me, so they can pick me up. That night I was taken in a jeep to waiting helicopter. I started to wake up when I say the helicopter and was struggling. Someone said to sedate the bitch. I was given a shot in the arm. I was taken to what I think is a base and told to put on fatigues very heavy and scratchy. I'm then ordered to run. I ran with several other soldiers in full gear, including an M16 rifle. We ran through caves and tunnels, all over this the underground bases. They treated me as if I was a soldier. I woke up exhausted in my bed with huge bruise on my legs. I woke up often with such bruises and scratches. I ended my friendship with her because she always seemed to be around when I was taken.

Later in 1999 I worked with Melinda Leslie on research for a "tell all" book. We interviewed MILAB abductees, both civilian and military. The following are all the things the Black Ops did to me that finally caused me quit my research into MK-Ultra, Targeted Individuals, Ritual Abuse and Super Soldiers. It started with many anonymous calls telling me to quit, throughout 1999 & 2000.

I believe the first warning that would be definitely related to the threats I had received, was on June, 26, 2000 at around 12:00 PM on a very foggy night. I had a very strange car accident with Melinda Leslie. I was driving my car on Rancho Santa Fe Road just outside town, when a bright light but it shinned in my eyes, blinding me and causing me to slam into the side of a hill. (I don't know what kind of car could have made such a bright light to blind me, since we had seen no cars on the rode).

I had to hit the hill because the alternative was to go off a pretty high cliff, which would actually have meant possible death. The air bags deployed so we were only slightly injured. Melinda received a bump on the knee and I wasn't hurt at all, except for some burns from the bags deploying.

The next morning at work somebody pointed out that my license plate was missing. So I went back to see if I could find it on the side of the hill. I parked my car on the side of the rode at the bottom of the hill. I took my keys and started walking beside the rode up the hill. A car went by me then I saw it speed back by me followed by a pickup truck. I found my license plate in the side of the hill and started back down the road. When I got close to my car I could see something glistening on the ground. But as I got, to my car I found that my window had been broken on the passenger side and upon opening the door and looking in, I saw that my purse was gone. OMG I felt pretty hopeless. My purse had my phone and my entire id in it and I didn't know what to do. I didn't want to leave the scene and no one else had sopped, since it wasn't a very well-traveled road.

However, I did not know but there had been an eye witness to the event. A man driving the pickup truck pulled up to my car. Came over excitedly to my car and proceeded to tell me was an eyewitness whole thing. He told me how a car had pulled out in front of him in such a fast manner, he had to almost stop. He saw my window broken and starting following the truck. He pulled up alongside of the truck and saw a man wrapping up his bleeding arm with a rag of some kind. He took a mental picture of the man and fell back behind him and took his license number make and model.

Then he returned to help me. He had called the police because they showed up right after.

Even though there was an eye witness and they caught the guy a few days later, none of my belongings were returned to me. My purse and everything in it was gone. I went to court when he was having his arraignment. The thief made a statement from the Judges acquisition. He said that he was an addict and said he was sorry he had broken into my car and stole my purse. The Judge asked where is her purse and belongings? The thief said he had sold my driver's license and social security card, credit cards and check book on the black market and had thrown my purse in a garbage can. He pleads guilty and was sentenced but what was really terrible and unfortunate for me. Before, I could get all of my accounts closed I had chargers and bounced checks all over the city. I was a victim of identity theft and it caused so many problems with my credit, for several years after.

I had much harassment from certain people but I believe it was the black ops and power elite. It was very obvious that they were following me as there were vehicles parked around my home. I was sure they tapped my phone calls. Often during my conversation with other people they would come on the line and make snide remarks and then hang up. Things would come up missing in my house.

My mail was tampered with my email was tampered with.

Melinda and I often had interviews with men and women for the book. In late 2000 we were still researching and interviewing lots of retired military and Special Forces for information for our book. I had quite a few interviews in my home so I didn't think anything of it when someone contacted me and said that he had been in the military in Special Forces that he had information for me and had much to tell me. I made an appointment for him to come to my house the next day.

He arrived at my house and rang my door bell. I opened the door and he sat on the couch and we started the interview. It seemed like there was no problem even though he was a large black man weighing about 250. As I interviewed him, he looked like he was getting more and more agitated and all of a sudden he starting acting real crazy. He said "you seem like a nice lady and I feel bad for you because they want you dead, since you won't shut up! He told me he was sent to kill me. I'm just following orders from the Major he's my commanding officer. He was just sitting there on my couch saying this to me.

I did some really quick thinking. I knew since he seemed unstable and crazy and acted pretty stupid, I might be able to bluff him, so this is what I did. In the most powerful and demanding voice I could muster, I stood up and paced back and forth in front of him and told him. "I also have a commander, he is a Colonel, my commander is above you Major in rank and my commander's orders are more important than you Majors. ' I told him he had to go back and check with his major to see which orders to follow, that all orders are to be canceled by my superior officer the Colonel.

Thank God, it worked I had confused him enough and I had bluffed him into leaving. Once he was gone out of site. I ran and jumped in my car and went to the police station and reported the threat. The police took my report and gave me mug shot book it seemed like a long time looking through the mugshots but I finally saw his face and pointed him out to the officer. The police officer told me that he was on parole from prison for sexual offences; he could not tell me exactly what type. I made a report and then went to court and got a restraining order against him. I went home with high hopes they would catch him and this would be over.

He came back to my house the next evening and pounded on my door, since my car was in the garage, I hoped, since he could not see my car, he would thing I was not home. I never let him know I was in there. Went to my bedroom and called the police. I was hiding in my bedroom for what seemed like forever, for him to go away. I thought he must've left when he heard siren. The police came to my house and took my statement and told me not to worry that that they had his name and description and knew where he worked, they said don't worry we will get him. A few days later the police contacted and told me. I would not have to worry about him anymore. That he had violated his parole and had been sent back to prison.

There are times when I would meet complete stranger and they would say things to me like aren't you worried that they'll come after you. Even in dating life I had odd warnings. The men I met and dated always seem to be in the military. I had on occasions where I think I might even turned one of their Special Forces guys into being my friend. He also said aren't you worried about messing around with such things. I like you and you really need to get out of this. You know I don't want you hurt you're messing with some pretty powerful people out there. But I continued on my project.

The next and more physical warning I had was on August 20, 2000. Melinda had stayed over at my condo in La Costa, Ca because we were working on a book and we were going to have an interview on the Art Bell, Dream Land radio show with Roger Siegel. The interview was going very well when all of a sudden I was asked have you ever seen different looking aliens besides the grays in the underground bases.

I started to share my experience about the reptilian was cut off. Melinda's phone did not disconnect so she continued the interview. It took a good 20 minutes for me to get back on the phone and by then the interview was almost over. We didn't really think too much of it I thought it was kind of odd that it wasn't able to speak about reptilian's on the radio but there was much else we can do so we went ahead and went to bed. We worked on our research the next day and that night Melinda received next day in it was late so Melinda stayed another night.

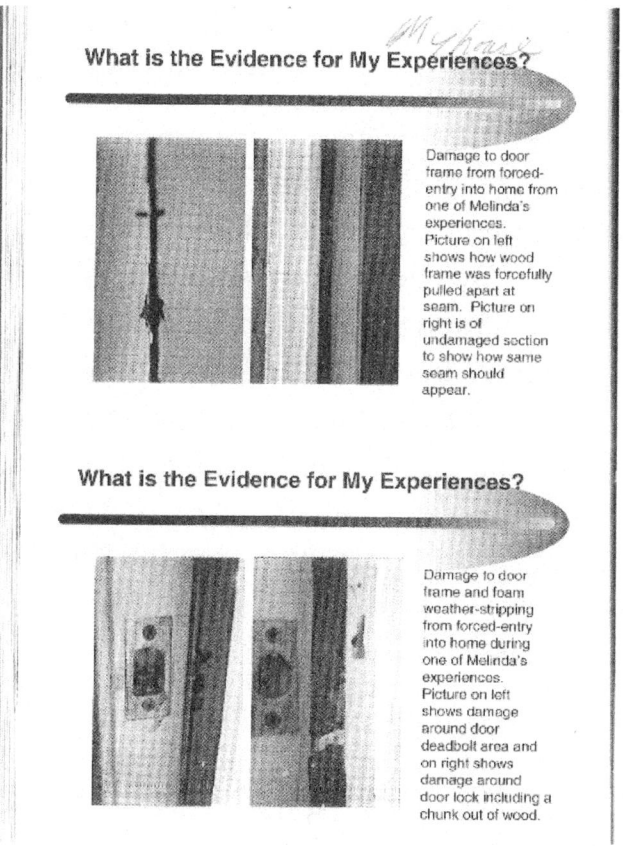

What is the Evidence for My Experiences?

Damage to door frame from forced-entry into home from one of Melinda's experiences. Picture on left shows how wood frame was forcefully pulled apart at seam. Picture on right is of undamaged section to show how same seam should appear.

What is the Evidence for My Experiences?

Damage to door frame and foam weather-stripping from forced-entry into home during one of Melinda's experiences. Picture on left shows damage around door deadbolt area and on right shows damage around door lock including a chunk out of wood.

We woke up the next morning and noticed that my coffee table hand been broken. Melinda was sleeping on the couch and she did not remember falling on the coffee table or breaking it. It was very odd because there had to be a reason how my coffee table had gotten broke. I thought that she might have been sleepwalking and broke it but she couldn't remember. She had to go back home to Laguna Hills. I really felt uncomfortable and uneasy feeling. So I went and had a regression done. I found out later that she had the same very uneasy feeling about that night but we couldn't put her finger on it. That's odd that she's in Laguna Hills and I was in La Cost we both feeling the same very creepy feelings.

We had some odd conversations about how something was wrong. We decided to get hypnotized, so she did hers with her therapist in Laguna and me with my therapist here. In regression we both found out about the night. We both saw group military black ops, in black uniforms and night vision goggles. They had come into my condo and had abducted us. I had been taken out of my bed by two men in night vision goggles and dark uniforms. I was feeling very drugged and could not walk.

The men had a hold each arm and I was virtually carried me down the stairs to a waiting van. She had found out in her hypnosis a very similar experience. She had been woken up by them when they were picking her up off the sofa, she felt drugged and dizzy and had fallen on to my coffee table breaking it. They had put us had put us in the van feet to heads, so if we woke up we couldn't talk. I also feel they did it that way so we would be confused and not know where they had taken us.

The ride in the van was very hard. I kept waking up and going back to sleep and waking up and falling back to sleep but Melinda remembers more than I do. The next thing I remember is the van coming to a stop there was a light coming through the window of the front passenger side seat the next thing I remember I was being dragged out of the van and taken into a building. To me it looked like an airplane hangar. We were both taken to different rooms and interrogated by humans in a dark uniform.

The room I was in had everything seemed to be in the dimply lit almost dark but there was a very bright light one me, which blinded me so I could not make out the faces of other people in the room. I could see and man in uniform at the door just standing with a large weapon that appeared to be a machine gun. I sat up. I was on a table, the kind you see in a doctor's office but metal. There was a man in another in uniform. I feel he was an officer.

He told me. "You stupid bitch we have told you to stop talking. You might think this is your mission but it is over now." "You will stop writing the book and stop lectures and never talk about it again. Go back home by use of a husband and get married and forget about all of this because **it's not going to bring you any happiness**. While these with the same words that were sent to me to have times during threats of my life with this some kind of a trigger think it was. He went on to say, "to show you how serious this is I want you to meet someone else.' Then through the door and out of the darkness came a Draconian. He was close to 7 to 8 ft. tall with light greenish gold very scaly looking skin. He had what appeared to be like skin protruding at his shoulders over his back that could have been like wings or what was left of wings. He had a long tail that swished back and forth when we walked over to me.

He bent down and stared deep into my eyes. This was similar to other mind melt that I had experience with reptilian to the underground bases. But this was very different because the horrific vision that was put into my head terrified me. The image he put into my mind was a terrible vision of my family, my children and grandchild all being dismembered as I watched in horror as, black uniformed Ninja soldiers with long swords had chopped them up in front of my eyes.

I stood their helpless to stop them and it the most horrible sit I had ever seen. But there was one thing, that wasn't right. I could not hear anything no screams no noise came from this horrible pitcher. I thought to myself this is not real and I remember saying "is this real or Memorex". At that moment I came out of this hypnotic state. I broke his trance. I don't remember him leaving. I'm not even sure that there was really Draconian in the room at all. Was it possible I had been hypnotized by humans and there were no such draconian was ever there. It's possible that a human gave me a hypnotic suggestion to make me see the draconian and make me see this whole scenario. Melinda and my description of the Draconian differed somewhat. I don't know if it was just how we pictured and described it or if there were two of them or was it even real!

The Draconian I saw from the base during Melinda & my abduction

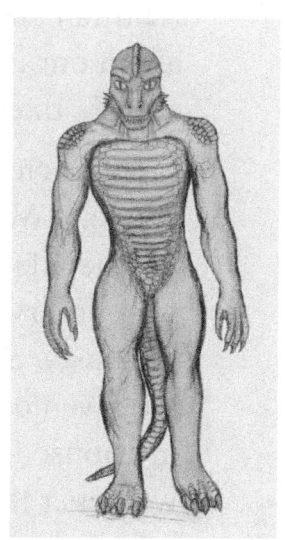

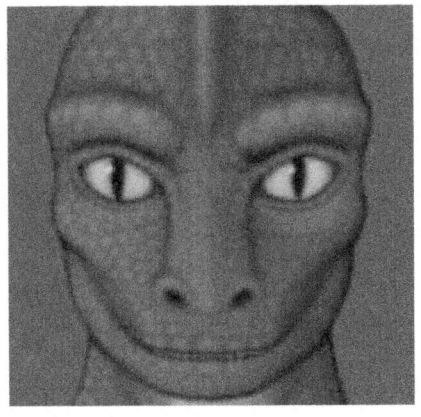

Description of Melinda's Draconian from the base

Melinda remembered in her regression that she had a very similar integration also with a Draconian, this was the first time she had ever seen a reptilian (Draconian). She told me he put an image of him attacking her, raping her and dismembering her. The odd thing was her draconian and my draconian were similar but our descriptions to the artist David Chace were quite different. We had the same forensic artist do both pictures. David Chace is a very talented artist. He is the best at drawing reptilian aliens. We talked briefly over the phone about our individual regressions. Our stories corroborated each other.

I took pictures of door jams and the break in. (pic above.) We never talked to each other about the real details of that night until 16 years later. We were interviewed on the Aquarian Radio show by Dr. Sasha & Janet Lessin in June 2016. I know they wanted me to know that they could come into my house to take me anytime and could do whatever they wanted to me. We however did not quit our research and continued interviewing people.

In late 2000, Melinda and I attended the conference just after the abduction in San Diego. Melinda and I were talking with Dr. John Mack and Richard Hoagland about our research about the book and about all the problems that we had both had because of research for book. They both told us that this is a very important book and that you need to finish this book. You need to write this book. It will help so many people. So we decided that there was nothing that was going to stop us. We continued our research and interviewed lots of retired military and Special Forces for information for our book.

I talked to my kids and told them what the two researchers had said. I also told them about the threats I had received. I didn't want to frighten but I did tell them about the incident with the Draconian on the base. They told me that Mom this is important and you need to keep going with your research. We can take care of ourselves.

In late Nov, 2000 I got a call from a man who said he had been Special Forces. He said he had some real good information for me. I had learned my lesson from this other dangerous encounter. So from then on I would only do interviews in a public place, until I got to know them and find out if they were safe. I was to meet him in a restaurant bar. I waited he showed up in a green flight jacket with a Lt. Colonel emblem on the pocket.

The first words out of his mouth were, "So how is that cute little granddaughter of yours in _____ Nevada? She is 3 now, isn't she?" I knew I was in trouble. How did he know I had a granddaughter in _____ Nevada? I said "how would you know I have a granddaughter." He said, "We know everything about you and your little family." "We know your granddaughter's age yours sons age where they work, we know they routines and everything about them." They find people's bones in the desert all the time."

You think you're so smart little lady but you're not." "The people are not ready to hear what you have to say." But I said they have a right to know. He said, "What would happen if the masses knew that the aliens were real and that they could come and go as they chose and could abduct anyone they wanted to, without us being able to do anything to stop them". "The people would be terrified it would cause panic and cause everything to fail." The world is just not ready to hear this." "Little girl you need to stop what you're doing and go find a man get married and forget about all of this, and forget about all this." "**This is not going to bring you any happiness**." Once again that odd statement was made.

He then on left but I followed him out the door to see what kind of vehicle he was in. He saw I had followed him out. I guess that pissed him off. Because he proceeded to scream at me in the parking lot and said that "It would be harmful to my family if I continued on the path I was on". He said "it would be a shame if something happened to you or your family." He said "there is a big desert out there around Nevada" as he was getting into the car he screamed "Keep your f-----ing mouth shut." A couple in the parking lot heard him screaming and asked if I was OK, because they could see how shook up I was, he saw them and got in his black cobra and sped way.

On Dec 23 well driving home to ------- Nevada for the holidays I drove down the middle lane at 72 MPH with my Cruise control on. When I was ran off the road by an unmarked white van. A white van passed in the fast lane and disappeared out sight. Shortly after that I came up on a line of tractor trailers in the slow right lane. When all of a sudden the white van pulled from between two trucks and forced me off the road. I went down in the medium and my car went out of control and went up to oncoming traffic but I was able to get it under control and got back in the medium.

I thought to myself that I may die this time. But just then out of now where a cactus tree was in front of me. Everything was in slow motion and I came to a very soft landing on the cactus tree, which finally stopped the car. A trucker and his wife stopped to help me. He said they had seen the whole thing and could not figure what the white van was doing in their lane in the first place. He said it looked like it was intentional.

The trucker said "that was a fine piece of driving keeping, that fire-bird from flipping over. He said "he radioed ahead to other truckers get the license plate of the van and they had called the 911 for me. The damage to my car was not too bad, just the bumper was hanging off. There were dents on the front hood. It was a miracle that that cactus tree was there, because that is a stretch road where there are very, very few cacti. It's as if someone put it there for me to hit and stop my car. It saved my life most likely. Since I was unharmed even though I had my T Top open on my Firebird and branches from the cactus were in my backseat.

I had very few scratches my airbags had not deployed and I could drive my car. I did call my son and he came out and helped me by pulling off. The bumper, so I could drive. He followed me home to make sure I got to his house safe.

I spent the holiday with my family. I knew this time they were serious. I told my family that I had decided I was getting out before something happened to them. I told them I was going back and close my group and turn over all my interview tapes, interview notes, written material and all pictures and other research back to my research partner Melinda Leslie.

When I got back to San Diego I took my car into the shop for repairs and rented a car. I met with Melinda. Well needless to say I turned everything over to Melinda. I wished her luck and told her everything then headed to a friend's house to give him my books. While I was driving there a SUV blew through the red light and hit me broadside, spinning my car around. The guy who jumped out of the SUV was a large man with a military buzz haircut. He screamed at me, "that it was my fault and said you would have to take the blame." I knew something was fishy. Just then two people walking down a hill heard him yell at me came over to my car and said they would be my witness. The police came and did an investigation and talked with the eyewitness and issue a citation to him. Once again Angel with me I was not hurt but my car was un-drivable.

I stayed out of everything from that day on for almost 9 years. I never talked & to any of my friends or my colleagues in the research field. I closed my groups and never attending anything. I got away from it all. I tried to have a normal life but my heart was always wondering what if I had never left, we could had finished the book. I decided I needed to go on with my life. I continued on with my job working for a home builder, in my field as an executive administrator. I was just living life because I was happy to be alive. I thought it was last of it.

A year later in the end of 2002, I was trying to get on with my life and meet someone for a relationship. I met a guy on a dating site. We set up to meet at a golf driving course. As was my custom I only met men in a public place and only in the daytime.

When I got there he was drinking a cup of coffee. He asked if I would like one. He went to the snack area and bought the coffee out to me on the driving range. That was the last thing I remembered until I sort of woke up in the woods while he was raping me. But due to the drugs he had given me I could only scream on the inside. I could not fight him off I was unable to control my body or even move it.

The next thing I remember is I woke up in my car behind the wheel. He must of giving me a lot of drugs because I could not remember what happen to me until late that night. I was in a fog all day. I called my friend and she met me at a restaurant, I felt very strange but had no memory. As we talked I was having flash backs into the attack. I starting getting more flashes and pieced together my memories of what happened to me. Around 9pm we left and she took me to the police station.

After making a full report to the police they told me he had probably given me Ketamine Rohypnol or "roofies" (the date rape drug). The management/ (CIA) have used it within their mind control system. It is the most known of amnesia drugs. Rohypnol has been used because it renders its victims incapable of resisting, giving it the reputation of the "date rape" drug. A person can be incapacitated within 1 hour and it can last 8 hours and even as much as 12 hours. That is why it took me so long to get any of my memories. I was in a fog, until later then afternoon.

When I gave them the location of the attack, they looked at each and they said. "We are sorry but this is not our jurisdiction it had happen on the border of Carlsbad and they were Oceanside Police. They said they were very sorry but I had to go to the Carlsbad Police Department. I could not go through anything else that night. I went home and showered and cried. I did not go to the Carlsbad police department until the next morning.

The police said they did not have a rape kit at the station and he told me it was probably too late anyway. The policeman at Carlsbad Police Department was mean, cold and accusatory with me. He said "If you go on dating sites you had better expect to meet some perverts, you're asking for trouble." "It's your own fault." I left after filing a report, he had been cruel and heartless and no help to me.

I was called back by a detective a few days later. He told me I could press charges and go to court but since it was a date rape it was just his word against mine that it ever happened. He had no priors and had never been arrested, he was a solid citizen. He said that if I chose to go ahead with this that when I got on the stand in court, it could get very ugly. I didn't know I could go through that. I decided not to pursue it any longer, even though my Rape counselors said I should pursue it.

I am not sure if the government sent the rapist after me but I have always wondered. I went to extensive therapy and learned to deal with what he did to me. This was an awful thing to happen but I've had much worse done to me, like what had happened to me during my missing times for those years. My memories have been coming back.

I was a Monarch and in Project Talent; sex slavery, ritualistic abuse, and many other trauma based torture methods. I have done a lot of work on both missing times in 1968 & 1970 (each 7 - 9 month periods) I have a marriage I don't even remember but it is coming back too. I have gotten some of my memories back and I have received answers and now I realize what happened to me was so terrible; the rape brought it all back. Believe me when I say that what happened to me in those missing periods of my life was much worse than the rape. I will be writing about the missing years in my next book, Volume 2.

Miesha Johnston ~ Bio

Miesha Johnston is a Certified Hypnotherapist of AHA and specializes in Past Live Regression, Trauma Recovery Hypnosis, ADD & ADHD. She works with people who have had: ET Experiences, MILAB, MK-Ultra, Targeted Individual, Monarch, Montauk and Ritual Abuse. She is also a channel and offers private Multi-Dimensional Galactic Light Language Activation & Healing Sessions.

Miesha facilitates 2 monthly support groups in her private residence in Las Vegas, NV, and 2 weekly virtual support groups on the internet through Zoom for Starseed Awakening Support Groups. Miesha has a weekly radio show Starseed Awakening on KCOR Radio every Saturday at 12:00PM PST and is a panel member of the TV show, Transcending Realities on IVOLVE TV.

In 1991 Miesha founded the Star Family Contactee Groups now called Starseed Awakening. These groups are for people who are experiencer's: men, women, teens and children who are contactee/experiencer by ETs. She started the first teen and children's groups in the United States in 1994. Miesha was director of U.F.O.C.C.I.

(UFO Contact Center International) and Celestial Contacts of Nevada from 1989 to 1997. She was a working group member of Steven Greer's C.S.E.T.I. in Las Vegas, NV. She moved to San Diego in 1998 and was the Coordinator of the Art Bell Chat Club San Diego Chapter 1998-2001. Miesha has been interviewed on many radio shows including Art Bell's Dream Land and have spoken at UFO Conventions throughout California, Colorado and Nevada She conducted research with Melinda Leslie for a MILAB Book until 2001. Her story has been featured in a few books.

Miesha is a 2nd generational experiencer, MILAB and Mk-Ultra survivor. She had her first experience at age three. She has had numerous contacts and abductions and has been involved with at least 8 different alien types: Most extraordinarily, Miesha has had three missing times (each 8 months to year) as an adult due to being taken and used in the Monarch projects and project talent.

Websites:http://starseedawakening.org
https://www.facebook.com/groups/starseedawakening/
http://www.meetup.com/Las-Vegas-Psychic-Awareness-and-Starseed-Experiencer-Group/events/30931721/
starmiesha99@yahoo.com

In 1992 Miesha Johnston founded the Star Family Contactee. These groups are for people who are experiencer's: men, women, teens and children who are contactee/experiencer (abducted) by ETs. She started the first teen and children's groups in the United States in 1994. Miesha was director of U.F.O.C.C.I. (UFO Contact Center International) and Celestial Contacts of Nevada.

She was a working group member of Steven Greer's C.S.E.T.I. in Las Vegas. Miesha moved to San Diego in 1998 and was the Coordinator of the Art Bell Chat Club San Diego Chapter 1998-2001.

She has been interviewed on many radio shows including Art Bell's Dream Land and has spoken at UFO Conventions throughout California, Colorado and Nevada. She researched with Melinda Leslie for a MILAB Book until 2001.

Miesha's story has been featured in a two books. She is a 2nd generational experiencer. She had her first experience at age three.

She has, had numerous contacts and abductions and has been involved with at least 5 different alien types: grays, insectoids, mammalians, reptilians, and human looking groups. She has had many MILAB experiences and has been in the underground bases which include a black ops branch of our government and some Grey and Reptilian factions. She was born and raised in a MK-Ultra family started her trauma based training for Projcct Monarch at agc 3 and was put in to service at age 9. She has had three missing periods of time in her life extending to 8 months. During which time she has little or no memory of what happened. Including a wedding & husband she has no memory of at all.

I have 12 to 16 experiencer groups per month on an internet on google hangout and in my home. I'm working with some other people, on the Thrive at my Education – The Thrive School of Nevada will be a school to allow learning to happen naturally, and allow learning to happen at each child's individual pace. We will use strategies and methods designed to cater to the unique learning style of each child, with the understanding at each child learns differently and that not all children learn by the "One Size Fits All" approach, mandated by the common core curriculum in today's public education system.

Our school will nurture and educate children from Kindergarten to Grade12, also known as the "Star Children, Crystal Children, Indigo Children and Rainbow Children". We will have guidance instructors, not just teachers. This will provide a platform of knowledge, a place of love, equality, and nurturing of an individual child's unique abilities.

We believe these special children need an alternative to this current curriculum of schools today, with classes for the Star kids, allowing them to learn and to connect with their own identities, abilities, gifts, mission, imagination and higher consciousness.

In my many years as a support group facilitator, I have discovered techniques which will help the individual find their OWN answers transmute their fear and reach their own transformational path. I feel such a complete transformation in my life. I have been amazed by the changes in my life in the areas of my abundance, health and my well-being; you realize you truly are a "spiritual soul having a human experience".

Starseed Awakening Support Groups Organization
https://www.facebook.com/groups.starseedawakening

Miesha Johnston facilitates 16 Experiencer Support Groups each month, 2 are in a private residence in Las Vegas each month. The others are 4 times a week on the internet live chat, on Google Hangout

Miesha has lectured Super Soldier Summit, Mind Control Summit & UFOCON. She has written many articles and is currently writing her book telling her own story.

DETOUR: THE ABDUCTION EXPERIENCE OF MELINDA LESLIE AND TWO FRIENDS

Melinda Leslie

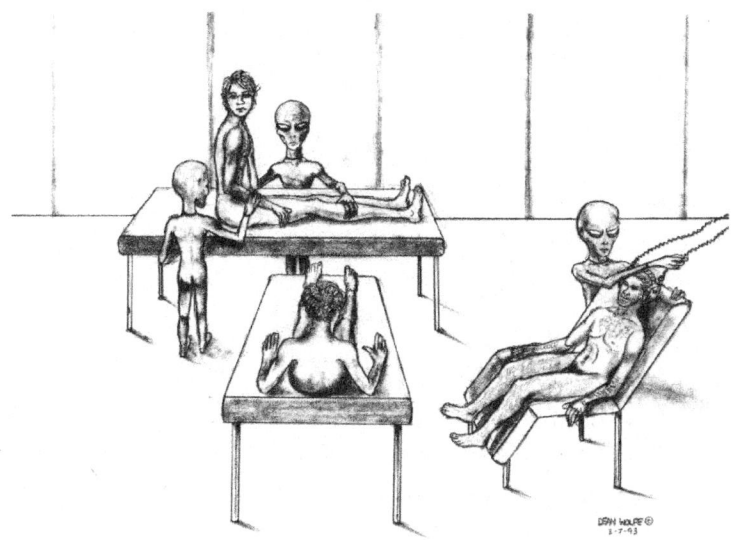

July 21, 1990 two male friends and I were abducted together while driving on a mountain road and experienced over 2 hours of missing time. The 3 of us each had some conscious memory and had separate hypnotic regressions for the details. The hypnotherapist later said we each remembered the exact same experience.

We are all UFO investigators and had left one of our homes at 10:00 p.m. planning on going sky watching at a local UFO sighting "hot spot" less than 2 hours away. Shortly after leaving we stopped at a drive-through restaurant for some quick food and drinks for the road. We had decided to take a route over the mountain because it was the quickest way. The beginning of the drive was uneventful and we were making good time since we wanted to get out to the location as soon as possible and due to our leaving late.

As we started up the mountain road and entered a forested area we started seeing a variety of animals; a deer, black dogs, and coyotes. Each of us remembered seeing a coyote in the road. At some point we started seeing lights off in the distance that we speculated may have been UFOs. The 3 of us started to argue about whether we were seeing UFOs in the sky to the right or the left of our car.

I was sitting in the back seat of our SUV and looking out the right side window. One of my friends was the driver and the other was sitting in the right front passenger seat. My friend in the right seat was shining a large spotlight up in the sky out his side window. We would often bring this along on our investigations in hopes of "calling in" a UFO and increasing our chances of having a sighting. This night it was to be a lesson in being careful of what you ask for.

As we argued about whether we were having a sighting or not and what side of the car it was on when there was suddenly three bright, blinding flashes of light inside and outside of the car and we all reacted saying "what the?!". I then noticed my friend on the right still had the spot light out his window so that wasn't the cause of lighting up the whole car. Then suddenly my friend who was driving slowed down the car and pulled it over to the right. I said "why are you stopping?" and he pointed out the front window and said; "because of that".

As we came to a stop, I saw a 4 foot tall gray alien being standing in front of the car. My friend driving later said the being, or some energy force, took over the car after the 3 flashes and brought the car to a stop, not him. He said the car was no longer under his control at that point. Then 2 alien beings came to the front passenger side door and opened it. My friend who was sitting there appeared to panic and a being touched him on his forehead and his head slumped down as if he was just "shut off".

Meanwhile another being had come to the driver's door, but that friend appeared to get out of the car on his own. I moved to the center of the back seat and then heard the car's back hatch door open behind me and suddenly I found myself floating up off my seat. I was paralyzed and laid out floating flat on my back over the seat and out the back hatch door and then set down on my feet, standing up, on the road, behind the car. Both friends saw this happen.

To the left of the mountain road the hillside dropped away becoming a high cliff and there hovered a large UFO craft. The artist simplified the craft for his drawing (attached), but the ship was actually layered, like a wedding cake, and was much larger than in the drawing. A ramp came down to the road from an opening in the side of the craft.

The driver had gotten out of the car on his own was now

walking onto the craft ahead of the being that was escorting him. My other friend was escorted by one alien to his side and another behind him. He was still slumped over and appeared to not be moving on his own. He would take a few steps and stop, then the being behind him would push on his back and he'd take a few more steps and stop again. This continued all the way up the ramp.

I was escorted by a being that took me by the hand and led me up the ramp and on board the craft. Once on board our clothes were removed and we stood there, naked, in front of each other.

Each of us recalled later how we were so concerned, not for our own wellbeing or embarrassment, but for each other's discomfort. While we weren't speaking during the event, we each later said we were trying to comfort each other with our eyes as if to say "it's okay that you are seeing me this way and don't be concerned for me, I'm okay."

We were each walked into an adjoining room where there were 2 examination tables and a large reclining chair, similar to a dentist's chair. My alert friend was escorted up onto one of the tables, the other was sat in the chair, and I was escorted up onto the other table. The beings preceded to vaginally remove eggs (ova) from me. This was an all-too familiar procedure for me. I've had this done in many of my abductions.

My friend on the other table was positioned in such a way as to give him a clear view of what they were doing to me. He kept turning his head away for my sake, but the beings kept forcing him to turn back and watch, but he wouldn't. Later he said the beings were trying to excite him so they could extract sperm, but that he was mortified for me and that the beings were frustrated at his refusal to look at me. The beings attempted to remove sperm but discovered he had a vasectomy. He said the beings questioned him and did not understand why he would do this to himself, that they were very perplexed by it.

Meanwhile, my friend in the chair had some kind of headpiece that looked like headphones placed over his head and ears. He just stared ahead, motionless, but would blink every now and then. After the beings were done with my procedure, they removed me front he table and escorted me to another room. This room was large and I was made to stand in the middle of it. There were at least 10 beings in this room and they formed a large circle around me.

A black metallic mesh bag was pulled over my head, shoulders, and upper arms, and then it was tightened below by chest as if a drawstring was pulled. This pinned my arms to my sides and restricted their movement. It was completely dark inside this thing and I couldn't see. Next thing I knew I was being pushed sideways and I started to fall over. I tried to move my feet to step out and catch myself, but my feet and legs wouldn't move. I was paralyzed again. This was very frightening because I realized that if I fell over I wouldn't be able to break my fall and I'd be banged up to say the least. I was scared to death.

Suddenly my leaning over was stopped in mid-air, by an energy force, and I started to go upright again only to then pass the standing position and start falling in the opposite direction. They then repeated this with my going back and forth. It started slowly without leaning me too far over, but then the speed and distance increased with each energy push. Each time I'd be pivoting and falling in a different direction. Eventually I fell so far over I was only feet from the ground before they'd "catch" me and send me in the other direction. I felt like one of those kids' blow-up clown punching toys.

This was a horrific experience and at first I was never sure if I was going to go crashing to the floor. I was screaming and begging them to stop. I was also getting sick to my stomach from the motion and completely terrified. It seemed to go on forever. I eventually realized they were not going to drop me and learned to relax with it. The less I resisted, the less distance they'd drop me and the more I relaxed, they'd slow down the process. Eventually I was left standing still.

They took the bag off my head and it took me awhile to focus my eyes and get my equilibrium back. The room was still spinning. I was pissed off at them for scaring me so bad and I said "what the hell was that? You could have killed me!" The beings offered a weak apology and said I had to learn that I could trust them and that they couldn't stop until I realized they were never going to drop me. I have a fear of heights and on this, and one other abduction, the aliens somehow knew it and knew they could push that button.

In retrospect, this was just like some corporate executive's training exercise where you fall back with your eyes closed and your coworkers catch you to build trust and teamwork. Accept this was a trust training exercise on steroids! I was still angry as they took me back into the other room. Later one of my friends said he had no idea where they took me, but that I looked really pissed when they brought me back. He saw that my face was bright red and tear-stained. He said he knew I was okay cause of the look on my face.

While I was out of the room from where my friends were, the beings gave my alert friend specific technical information. He later said they showed him how to build a small simple device that would detect the presence of a UFO by detecting a difference in the magnetic field around the device. The UFO detector had both a light and an alarm that would go off if the field was disturbed. You could set the device for the light or the sound to go off.

He later made these devices, gave them to UFO researchers, and sold them at conferences and events. While the devices did work, they often malfunctioned and eventfully he gave up making them. He always claimed the whole idea and design of the device came about in this experience during the time I was out of the room having my "trust" exercise.

Our other friend just sat in the chair the whole time, but eventually without his headset device on. He appeared to slowly regain awareness towards the end of the experience. It should be noted that during his multiple regressions for this event, from the moment the car stops, till the moment he got out of the chair, all he remembers is a violent spinning sensation that he's not been able to break through. This may be the product of his having been "shut off" to some degree.

We were all escorted out of this room and back into where are clothes were waiting. We were instructed to get dressed quickly and we did it on our own. We were escorted back down the ramp and over to the car. We each got into the car on our own, but with the beings directed us.

We were then paralyzed and each positioned as if moving a manikin into position, back to exactly how we were before the car was stopped. My friend who was driving drove the car off the shoulder back onto the road, I was in the center of the backseat, and my other friend had the spotlight placed back in his hands and was tilting it out his rolled down window once again.

We drove down the road, but my friend with the light couldn't get it back on. My friend driving said something about the radio scanners he had brought were not working, that they were making strange buzzing sounds. The one was explaining about the light, but the other thought he was talking about the scanners. The two of them argued about which equipment was not working before they figured out that ALL the equipment was having problems. We were each agitated and confused, but had no memory of what had just occurred. One moment we were arguing about what side of the car we were having a sighting on, and the next moment our equipment is going haywire and we don't know why. We didn't realize the 2 hours were seamlessly gone till a short time later.

We drove a short distance when suddenly all 3 of us talked about having to use a rest room. The driver couldn't wait so he pulled the car off the road into a large dirt turnout and both guys jumped out of the car to relieve themselves. Since this is never easy for girls, I opted for waiting till we got into town. We also all complained about being very thirsty. This is particularly strange because we had only stopped at the drive-through and had drinks only an hour earlier.

We drove into town and just off the freeway and because I couldn't wait any longer, we quickly found a convenience store. I darted in to use the restroom and all 3 of us bought large drinks. We sat in the car and each of us finished our drinks! We wondered why we were so thirsty when we had just had drinks at what should have been only an hour earlier.

We also discussed how odd it was that we weren't seeing any cars at all on the roads or people anywhere. We were in a normally busy area and it should only have been 12:00 midnight at the absolute latest. My friend in the driver seat then commented that it seemed much later and looked at his watch.

He then said; "you guys aren't going to believe this, but its past 2:30!!!" This didn't make any sense; it should only have been 12:00. We joked this off, yet we really couldn't account for the discrepancy or how the trip could have ever taken us so long. Especially since we had been in such a hurry!

We then drove and tried to find the location we had planned to go to, but got horribly lost and drove in circles arguing the whole time. After much frustration of driving nowhere, we eventually turned around and decided we were way too tired to do any sky watching. So, we started the drive home. My friend in the front passenger seat fell sound asleep.

We later learned that this was a very odd thing for him to do. It turns out that his whole life he's never been able to sleep in a car or any moving vehicle. Later his mother confirmed this for us, that to her frustration, even as a child he never slept in the car. Yet, this time he was out cold almost the whole way home! And, we took the long way back!

A few weeks later we drove this same route again during the day just to time how long it takes. And we've driven it many times since, but have found repeatedly that the whole drive should have taken about an hour and a half and not over 3 hours as it did that night. On that occasion the trip took a full 2 hours longer than it ever should have and the 3 of us experienced quite an unexpected detour.

Over subsequent days after the event our memories trickled back, but we agreed to never share what we remembered with each other till such time that we each had remembered as much as possible consciously, or received separate hypnotic regressions. It took months for each of us to get up the courage to get regressed and more months still to get through our hypnosis sessions. Eventually we met together, with our hypnotherapist, and she related to us that we had each recalled the identical same experience.

Melinda Leslie ~ Bio

Melinda Leslie ~ cell phone: 310-502-5398
Linnie@onebox.com

Melinda Leslie has been public with her own extraterrestrial and covert human abduction experiences for over 26 years. She researched a covert-ops military involvement in abductions for 25 years, and is currently writing a book detailing her research. Her research and personal experiences have been featured in over 20 books by prominent authors in ufology.

Melinda has lectured for numerous organizations including the International UFO Congress, multiple MUFON chapters, the X-Conference, Contact in the Desert, the Bay Area UFO Expo, UFO Con, UFO Expo West, The Whole Life Expo, and more. She has been a guest on numerous popular radio shows including as a repeat guest on *Coast-to-Coast AM*, and appeared on several television shows.

Melinda has also been a researcher and investigator in the field of ufology for over 27 years and in the paranormal field for 35 years. She is now the Director of UFO Sighting Tours in Sedona, Arizona, conducting over 700 tours with the use of military Generation III Night Vision Goggle equipment and spiritual intuitive consultations. For more information please visit www.UFOSightingTours.com

5 UFOs flying in formation as seen through Night Vision Goggles

Research: The Covert Program of Reverse-Engineering Extraterrestrial Abductees (MILABs): The Experiences, Evidence, and Implications

Melinda Leslie's latest research is on how covert human agency programs are reverse engineering extraterrestrial abductees for information to be used in both extraterrestrial (ET) technology and covert-ops personnel development programs. She explains how the management of ET information includes the monitoring, re-abduction, interrogation, and recruitment of alien abductees into covert programs, equating it to just as the covert-ops military personnel gather and reverse-engineer ET craft, they also gather and reverse-engineer the abductees.

Also called MILABs (military abductions) these experiences are abundant with evidence and also serve to demonstrate some of the implications and limitations for any official UFO Disclosure process.

Melinda's research covers detailed accounts of covert human agency abduction experiences and the covert-ops' attempt to learn the ET's motives and technology, abductee genetics, and psi (paranormal) abilities through these events. Melinda investigates startling new developments, evidence for the involvement, and the detailed experiences of those involved.

THE SOUTH POINT UFO EXPERIENCE

Barbara Jean Lindsey

After assuring my teenage son that my new friend, Patty, who was visiting from the Mainland and I would be home no later than midnight, we both jumped into the convertible and waived our exuberant good byes. We were off to visit a famous local spot, South Point, Maui, Hawaii--the southernmost tip of the island and the most southern point of land of the United States. On second thought, it was Patty's idea to seek out this desolate and isolated part of the island. This excursion, unbeknownst to us, would spark both our awareness of UFO's, up close and comfortable, 3D style, that is and expand our consciousness.

About 45 minutes later we pulled off the main highway and began our 15-mile trek down a narrow one way road with open expanses of cattle land on each side. Down the bumpy and dusty road, we flew singing and having a grand old time. When we arrived at the end of the fork in the road, we went left and parked our car just in time for a beautiful Hawaiian sunset, as we looked out into the great expanse of sea. We were getting ready to go home after a short walk and talking to the local fishermen of the day about what they had caught. The local fisherman at windswept "Ka Lae" or what the locals call, South

Point, we were told, just wouldn't let us go home because they explained that their luck had been rotten all day and nobody had caught any fish, until we showed up. Patty and I had suddenly become their good luck charms. Since we arrived the fish were almost jumping onto their hooks they all jokingly reassured us. As soon as the fishermen would cast their fishing rods down the deep 40-foot cliff side and into the dark rough ocean water noisily crashing below, invariably a large flapping fish would be drawn up the dark cliff and into their roughhewn hands.

There were about five to seven local fishermen in total, don't remember exactly how many were present that night, as it was getting very dark except for a few lanterns scattered about to help the fisherman bait their hooks. I got the sense that everyone knew everyone like family, as they teased one another and joked with each other in an easy familiar nature. We stood out like a sore thumb, as my friend, Patty was tall, shapely and very Nordic looking, with piercing blue eyes and long blond hair that she had in a ponytail with a baseball hat. I look somewhat more native, with long brown hair and large green eyes, on the more voluptuous side, wearing a traditional sarong and a big smile.

We were talking about nothing special and it was getting dark, when one local fisherman, by the name of Jimmy, offered us each a beer and motioned for us to sit down near him. As we all faced the sea into the darkness,

Jimmy explained that if you looked out toward that very cliff during the day you would fly right into Antarctica, if you were a bird, as South Point and Antarctica were exact opposite land masses from each other. We were all in a very relaxed state and having a good time. Fake sipping my beer, to be friendly, I became enthralled with Jimmy's stories about the local history.

Then off into the distance, suddenly floating up above, in the middle of the u-shaped harbor, a massive group of clouds appeared out of nowhere, instantly like magic. First there was nothing but darkness and then boom they were there! Perfect clouds, like someone took a gigantic can of whip cream and briskly shook it up and poured a perfect dense string of puffy clouds directly across the dark skyline. They began to move very quickly, like out of control, like the winds of a mighty sailing ship bursting them forward aimed directly toward us. What an incredible sight to behold.

At the very bottom edge of the clouds appeared a large round circle to the left and then in perfect sequential order to the right, appeared a smaller circle, then another and another, each descending in size but in a perfect line, from left to right. The circle windows were like taking a silver dollar, then a fifty-cent piece, then a quarter, then a nickel, then a penny and lastly a dime laying then out in a gentle half circle shape in a perfect line order. I could see just sneaking out below the perfectly transcending circle windows was a shiny metal disk. I forgot to mention that I could see the metallic disk without any problem as it was reflected by the bright light of the silvery moon. The moon was shining like an intense flash light on the entire scene. It was a spaceship, just like I had seen from the 1960 and 70's TV shows, like "Lost in Space and "Star Trek." In shocking disbelief, I thought to myself, oh my God, it is a space ship and it is coming right at us!

The spaceship zoomed over our heads and as I stood up and turned my head to the right to begin to watch it pass overhead, I looked up and saw it was moving at lightning speed and at the same time in slow motion directly over my head about the distance of the Empire State Building in New York, if you were standing on the sidewalk looking up to the top. Then like a split second, that is the last that I remember of the UFO.

The UFO was out of sight and I am now standing on my own and facing the cliff, staring out into the darkness. I recover from the shock and begin to look around and see everyone is standing up as in a daze, just like me, not moving but beginning to look around, trying to make everything familiar again. I am the first to shout out "Did anyone else see what just happened?" Everyone began to talk at once and we all agreed very quickly that we had just witnessed a real, live UFO. Wow, everyone was shaking their heads in disbelief and trying to figure out what to do. "Is everyone ok?" I asked. I am ok. Are you ok, Patty? Patty was ok. What just happened? Then everyone became rather silent again and just stood there much in shock and still dazed from the whole experience.

When suddenly, we heard a man's voice shouting at the top of his lungs from behind us, "Did you see what just happened?" "Did you see the spaceship? We all turned around and faced the open fields behind us and saw a bent over old man with a long gray hair in a ponytail dressed in khaki pants and an army fatigue shirt bounding down the foot path hauling his fishing pole and tackle box in one hand and shakenly carrying a bouncing lit lantern next to him.

We all shouted back in unison, that yes, indeed, we all saw the UFO. 'Thank God!" bellowed the old fishermen. "I thought I was seeing things and maybe going nuts in my old age." We all assured him that he was, "ok," and he laughed a gentle laugh and let out a great sigh of relief in the knowing that he had not been alone in his UFO experience.

Everyone began to pack up rather quickly and we all decided without saying it out loud to one another that it was high time to get out of dodge, as nobody wanted to be in the direct line of fire from a spaceship again. Patty and I nodded at one another telepathically and began to walk back to our convertible. We gave our brief goodbyes and everyone acted as if nothing unusual had just happened. We couldn't get out of there quick enough, as we sped off down the bumpy road once again.

As we were driving down the long narrow road back to Kona about 1/2 way there, Patty and I continued to be unusually silent. It felt like I was in the middle of nowhere with pitch darkness on both sides of the road. I could barely see anything past the car headlights as the road became suddenly so thick with fog. Patty turned on the radio, but there was nothing but static.

When suddenly a very tall white metal column appeared like out of nowhere off to the left of us giving off an eerie high pitched sound. Immediately, Patty and I both screamed out with all our might blood curdling screams and then we were both quite relieved to see that it was only a windmill.

Relaxed, we both began to laugh and swear. We agreed that we had enough surprises for a life time, but still didn't talk about what just happened. We were certainly glad to pull off the foggy South Point road and onto the normal highway in the direction of Kona to a safe and sound familiarity.

Afterwards, there were several facts to substantiate our UFO evening of peculiarities. Patty and I both discovered that we had unusual sunburns on our face, chest and uncovered arms. Funny, because neither one of us had been out in the sun for days before the UFO event. The local Hawaiian paper ran a small article the next day about several local Kona people witnessing UFO's flying overhead in the nighttime sky that very same night of our group UFO experience in the direct vicinity of South Point.

I am sure that we had missing time, because I had made a promise to my son to be home by midnight but it was about 4:00AM or so in the morning when Patty and I had gotten back and everyone at the house had been worried for our safety. So much so, that they considered calling the police. Patty and I thought we were a wee bit late, but not alarmingly late. To our surprise, it just didn't seem like we had been gone that long.

When Patty and I screamed bloody murder that night, when we were surprised by the windmill, was what I consider a highly unusual response. We are both very independent females and I know it takes a lot to get me afraid and to scream out in such terror, is not like me at all. It didn't make sense. What had happened that had frightened us so terribly to give us each such a knee jerk screaming reaction?

Had we been possibly taken aboard the UFO somehow and had our memory of the experience blocked? What did happen during that missing time?

The next year I went back to South Point to check out the exact location of the UFO group sighting. Determined to get to the bottom of the experience, I went late at night. I tried my best to get some answers and attempted to reenact the event, but never had any luck. I went back every year for several years, to the exact spot, hoping to see someone that I recognized from that fateful UFO evening. I continued over the years to return but without any luck. I lost touch with Patty and never saw her again after she flew back home to California. What was I searching for? Some answers to what? I always inquired about the whereabouts of the local fisherman named Jimmy, but no luck there either.

Over the years, traditionally, I would ask the fishermen there at South Point, if they had seen any ships lately? Usually, they would look at me with a quizzical shake of the head and respond with a quizzical and resounding" no." time and time again.

But, on one occasion, a fisherman did tell me that, yes, indeed, he had seen a ship. It was a very old, old ship. He explained in detail that he was alone fishing late at night when a dense fog landed suddenly across the air with the winds slowing down to almost a stand still.

As the fog parted in the middle of the harbor (the exact location where we had seen the UFO appear), the most magnificent old crafted sailing ship with all the masts flying high, majestically sailed below in the dark water like a dream. He said that it was truly remarkable and the joy of the site of it was instilled into his mind like it had just happened yesterday when in fact, the incidence had occurred many years back. He seemed relieved to finally tell his true experience to someone who listened with honest respect.

Was it merely a coincidence that the old man's experience of the ship and the spaceship I had encountered were in almost the same spot? This made me wonder. Was this area possibly an interdimensional portal?

I did discover that there were several Heiaus or temples at South Point and many old cultural relics remained although worn into a mysterious timelessness by the unforgiving pounding of the incessant winds. The native Hawaiians considered South Point a sacred place to be honored and respected. It was supposedly the spot where the Polynesians first arrived on the island.

How did I fit this UFO experience into my reality? First, I will tell you what I didn't do. I didn't go into denial and pretend it didn't happen. I wanted to meet it head on, process the experience and learn from it. I didn't want to talk it away, by telling my true story of what happened and then let someone listening to my story, try and convince me that I was either, crazy, drunk or on drugs.

I know myself well enough over the years, what the truth is and what a lie is. I did not and will not tolerate being discriminated against. I think the listeners of my story were just trying their best to heal me and at the same time weave my experience into their own reality while sometimes inciting a negative reaction. I was not regressed to obtain the memory of the missing time, for some reason, whenever I look at doing that, every part of my being, says," no." I will let sleeping dogs lie for the time being.

That South Point UFO experience helped me to acclimate and then expand my consciousness in my relationship to UFO's and extraterrestrials even more than before. I have acclimated in a positive way, as I do not get bothered anymore by people who may discriminate and have judgment on my story. It is a free world and they are welcome to their opinions.

Now, I do ask them to keep an open mind about my UFO experience and it is not unusual for them to begin to share with me an extraordinary experience that they have had and perhaps never told anyone about before. Energies are exchanged, much healing occurs, and our consciousness continues to grow due to the sharing of these true experiences.

Nowadays, I am very comfortable living in a world that is full of extraordinary surprises with uncontrollable, magnificently unknown and unchartered experiences including but not limited to UFO sightings and ET's. I believe someday, sooner than later, it will not be such a big deal to see spaceships flying overhead, as it will be a normal part of our reality, like the rising of the sun or the setting of the moon. We will take it for granted. My hope is that these experiences of UFO sightings and meetings with ET'S will aid us as a species to continue to expand our consciousness and re-discover the true nature of our relationship with our beautiful planet within the mysterious cosmos.

Dying For the Light Paperback – May 31, 2016
By Barbara Jean Lindsey (Author)

An inspiring autobiography of one woman's Near Death Experience and transformation from average mother of three to galactic ambassador, Barbara Jean had it all; former homecoming queen, businesswoman, mother of three… but she always wanted to know if there was more… In 1989, she got her answer; after full-body channeling an ancient Egyptian being, her lungs collapsed, killing her in front of a live audience.

As her body lay in a coma in the ICU, her spirit was transported to a UFO over the Earth. "Dying For the Light" is Barbara Jean's true autobiography of her journey through life as a seeker of truth, her transformation after her Near Death Experience, and the details of what happened to her body and spirit during her death and return: what it felt like to be dead, the teachings she received from the Galactic Council, fighting to return back into her body, waking up again and re-acclimating with society afterward.

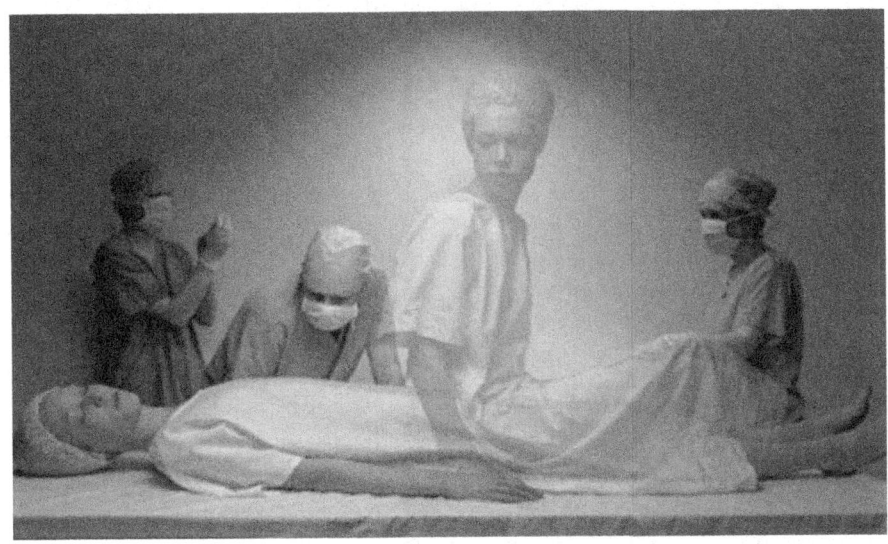

Barbara Jean Lindsey ~Bio

Barbara Jean Lindsey is an international intuitive consultant, holistic life coach, author and inspirational speaker. She is an international seminar trainer, Certified Fire Walking Instructor, Certified Medical Hypnotherapist, Qui Gong Medical Practitioner, Level II Reiki Initiate, 25-year Interfaith Minister and a Sister of Avalon.

In 1989, Barbara Jean had an extraordinary Near-Death-Experience; after full-body channeling an ancient Egyptian being, her lungs collapsed, killing her in front of a live audience. Over the next few days she fought for her life (on the physical plane, spiritual plane and beyond). Barbara Jean's story, journey and Transformation are chronicled in her autobiography, "Dying for the Light."

https://www.amazon.com/Dying-Light-Barbara-Jean-Lindsey-ebook/dp/B01GWONGJ4/ref=sr_1_1?s=books&ie=UTF8&qid=1485147666&sr=1-1&keywords=dying+for+the+light

Following her NDE, Barbara Jean has appeared on numerous television, radio, online and live event programs. She hosts the weekly "Cosmic Oracle Show" on the Revolution Radio Network on Tuesdays 9:00AM PST where listeners who have experienced something beyond themselves; from the Extra-Terrestrial (UFO and ETS) to the Spiritual (OBE's and Altered States) can call in and share their stories and she gives free psychic readings to callers.

Barbara Jean has hosted the Cosmic Cafe at the yearly Contact in the Desert Conference in Joshua Tree where contactees can share their stories publicly in a respectful and honored space.

She is the Dean and Founder of Esoteric University, an online mystery school for metaphysical studies. www.EsotericUniversity.com

Barbara Jean has sponsored and facilitated the annual "Heart of the Cosmic Woman" Conference, a gathering of women that empowers, inspires and heals women through celebrating the Goddess for over 15 years. Barbara Jean has been a professional intuitive consultant since her NDE over twenty-five years ago. She's available for private readings via phone or Skype.

Barbara Jean currently lives with her son, daughter-in-law and grandson in Altadena, California, where she pursues her passions in the arts, history, UFO' & ET research and antique collecting. She still loves nachos.

www.BarbaraJeanLindsey.com

THE STORY BEHIND THE FORGOTTEN PROMISE
Sherry Wilde

Why would a seemingly sane middle aged woman publicly confess to consorting with extraterrestrials? This lady had a marriage, children, successful business and a very respectable reputation for being reliable and trustworthy. Did she have a need for attention? Did she slip over the edge into insanity or become delusional? The answer is no. So why? What motivates someone to put it all on the line….risk everything, and for what? The ridicule that comes with the proclamation that you are in contact with aliens is not a pretty ride. You are attacked, snickered at, judged and avoided. Your integrity is questioned and the losses are beyond any possible gain…no, there is no rational explanation for this lady to make such a proclamation.

Or is there?

I am that lady and I went public with my lifelong ET contact in 2013 when my book, The Forgotten Promise, was published. So why did I do it?

The answer is even harder to believe than is my declaration of alien contact.

Those who investigate and work in the ufology field call

me an abductee. That is, I am a person who is taken against their will by beings from another world and subjected to psychological and physical testing. In other words, I am a victim. It was a very challenging label for me to wear when I first awakened to my experiences. Like many who have had these encounters, the memories are blocked and all you are left with are scattered, nonsensical pieces of a puzzle that don't fit together.

I got my wake-up call in August of 1987, during the Harmonic Convergence when I was compelled to stay home from work and sit on the hilltop overlooking our house. At the time it just felt like a meaningful few days of rest and appreciation, but I now know I was downloaded with the outline of the mission I was about to commence. This "download" was kept securely locked away and I had no conscious memory of it until many years later. In a few weeks my contact with the group of ET's I now refer to as "my guys" started in earnest. This contact- occurring during one of the most active periods of UFO sightings in the world- brought the Center for UFO Studies into my community, and eventually to me.

My life was thrown into a downward tumble of confusion and chaos as I was forced to believe and accept the most ridiculous thing I could ever have imagined…..that I was being abducted by aliens. I fought it tooth and toenail. I tried to find a doctor who would diagnose me as mentally ill….anything was better than having to accept that something as terrifying, as outlandish, as bizarre as this….could be real.

My life fell apart. I was sent adrift with no one and no thing to hold onto. I didn't have a strong religious foundation- I'd left the church, in disgust, when I was 15, finding all the guilt that was heaped upon us unbearable. I turned to my dad who had always had the answers and found him stone silent in the face of my inquiries and pleas. My husband left me. I couldn't work due to the stress. I was being taken by these beings several times a week- sometimes twice in the same day. This period of intense activity and interaction with them lasted around 18 months. They were teaching me things and training me for a time that was soon to come…a time they referred to as "The Great Earth Changes".

In late 1989 they appeared to leave my life. And as ridiculous as it sounds, I found myself missing them. That was disturbing, but with their absence I was better able to see the interactions from a slightly different perspective- one that wasn't tainted with so much fear. Eventually I put it behind me. Well, as much as it is possible to put such a thing to rest and I lived a relatively normal life for the next 20 years.

In 2009 my guys showed up in my bedroom in the middle of the night. I must have been in an altered state because I was just as calm as could be, as I looked at him and said, "What are you doing back here?" And he informed me, quite brusquely, that I'd been told about the

Earth Changes that were coming and we were in the midst of that now…and there was work to be done! We talked long into the night and he downloaded a lot of information to me. His visits continued and eventually tapered off to sporadic visits for the next several years.

It was during that period of time I found myself writing the book and being pushed to have it published. Make no mistake; I was not a willing participant in sharing my story with the public. Even with the awareness of all that had occurred and was occurring, I wanted no part of it. I wanted a normal life, but that was not to be.

Eventually I came to understand that I really had no choice. It seems I had made my decision long before I arrived on this planet. As part of my awakening experience I was remembering events prior to my birth. I saw that this was the course I had chosen for myself as a volunteer. This was my job….my mission. I came here, along with several other million souls to assist Gaia with her ascension. I had charted this course along with my Higher Self and by so doing had relinquished my rights to have a normal life.

So why does a seemingly sane middle-aged mother, and now grandmother, talk openly about her ET contact? Because it is time. Your cosmic family awaits your return and yearns to see you released from the shackles of imprisonment that have held this planet in a low frequency for so long. I talk about my contact experiences in an effort to spark a remembering in you. A remembering that we are not alone....that we have not been abandoned or forgotten.

Sherry Wilde ~ Bio

Sherry Wilde was living an idyllic life as a wife, mother and business owner until 1987 when her community experienced a UFO flap that was considered one of the most active in the world. No one could have ever guessed the unbelievable turn of events that would occur over the next 18-24 months as Sherry was forced to accept her involvement in a phenomenon that was totally unknown to her. Faced with the indisputable evidence that she was experiencing contact with extra-terrestrial beings was astonishing to this pragmatic and levelheaded woman of 37, but to learn her contact had been ongoing for her entire life almost pushed her over the edge.

Sherry spent the next several years of her life trying to exonerate the experiences from her mind and did her best to return to a normal life, but when heavy contact started again in late 2009, after several years of relative peace, she could no longer ignore it. Inexplicably she found herself writing a book about the encounters as her memory opened up to the past events and the teachings these beings had imparted to her. Overcoming her fear and learning the truth of her involvement with these ultra-dimensional beings became her life goal. She now accepts the truth of these encounters and has cooperative contact on a regular basis with the beings she affectionately refers to as "her guys."

Sherry has had an overwhelming amount of physical contact with beings from an alternate reality and has worked her way through the layers of disbelief, fear, confusion and ridicule. She found support and answers in places she never expected and through that process began to remember the truth of who she is. In this lecture she shares highlights and intimate details of that journey and talks about the differences between being an abductee and a volunteer.

www.TheForgottenPromise.net

Sherry Wilde was born & raised in southwestern Wisconsin and continues to spend the majority of her time there.

She operated a successful real estate business specializing in sales, land development and commercial renovations until the recession hit. Still somewhat active in real estate, she prefers to spend her time traveling & lecturing about her contact experiences in an effort to shed new light on the subject.

The Forgotten Promise tells the story of my lifelong interaction with beings of another dimension....or world. The memories of these encounters were buried deep within my subconscious mind until 1988.

It was then that a UFO flap occurred in my community bringing investigators from the J. Allen Hynek Center for UFO Studies to look into what was happening. Like many people, I could not and would not accept that such a thing as alien abduction was even plausible. Now, after having many years to adjust, grow and learn about this phenomenon, I must ask how is it possible to not believe that there is life "out there".

The universe, or multiverse, as I've come to understand it, is infinite. Think about that for a second. **It is mathematically impossible for us to be alone in the cosmos.** From there it is only a short step to recognizing that superior life forms are bound to exist and those life forms would have an interest in studying other life forms, just as we, one day will do. That is, if our species survives long enough to master space travel.

I've had the privilege of living an extraordinary life and learning from beings that exist in a realm quite different from the limited one we do.

I am now able to say that I am extremely grateful for these experiences, although it was not always so. The lessons they taught me, the things they showed me, the profound teachings & the high level of peace that is prevalent when in their company gives me hope for our planet. Knowing we are not alone and that we live in a universe governed by love is comforting.

LEVITATING BABY
Janet Kira Lessin

To be or not to be? I couldn't relate to my body. I just didn't get what it meant to be human. I visited my growing fetus after conception. I found it boring. Yes, it felt nice floating in a warm womb. Mother's heartbeat felt peaceful and welcoming. I felt a deep affinity for my new friend the placenta who loyal, always there, kept me company. With nothing to do, I felt bored out of my mind.

My parents-to-be traumatized by WWII and the depression lacked intellectual depth and didn't seem all that interesting. My mother had mixed feelings about her pregnancy, forthcoming birth and my life with her and my future family. Conflicted she had ongoing morning sickness, vomiting all the time which made her resent me even more. My father, shell-shocked from the war, had little to no opinion regarding my coming into the world. He worried about another mouth to feed as he didn't make much money as a mailman.

Years later Dad told me that "You were an accident. Most children born in the 50s were accidents." He made sense because the pill and other convenient forms of birth control emerged much later in the 60s. But I still felt shocked, sad, unwanted and ultimately unloved.

I almost left and if I had I would have stayed away for good. I talked to my guides, higher self and soul family. A couple of times I thought I'd made a mistake, that I needed to start over, chose another body.

They kept reassuring me that I really needed to stay true to my choice and get into being that babe forming in Mother's womb. I couldn't relate. Did I really agree to join as one with that thing that didn't look like much more than a blob?

I fast forwarded in time to see how this life turned out. I saw love, romance, passion, good times and bad and realized I fulfill my commitment and accomplish all my goals. Stars align; the cycles run their course to reveal I'm on the best possible timeline. I win the cosmic lottery and hold a pair of front row, center seat tickets for the Greatest Show on Earth… ever! Not only that, my twin flame/soul mate joins me and together we usher in the Golden Age of Aquarius. Bingo! Who could ask for anything more?

I witness and experience exciting times, the best and

worst of times which makes them unlike any other times and at the same time very similar. I looked at how this life correlated with my past lives and simultaneous incarnations. Yes, this body matched perfectly. This time and these experiences truly served me and the highest goals for all.

But still, I hesitated. With intensive apprehension my heart raced in abject fear. I wondered if I can really do what I promised I'd do.

At six months I struggled to get on my feet. My tiny hands grabbed tight on the wooden bars of my crib and pulled till at last I found the angle and correct balance for my feet to position beneath my body and I stabilized enough to remain standing.

Out of breath, my heart raced, I saw the world through my baby eyes for the first time. I looked out those eyes previously, for short bursts as per the agreement made before my birth. I had to agree to certain rules in order to earn a body in the first place. After all, I had a commitment to the body in which I shared consciously. My body and I exist in a symbiotic relationship and while for the duration of the experiment called life, we shared consciousness and knew our oneness.

Two separate beings joined by the process of life, felt like one. I felt responsible for my body as it contained programming within its DNA that I had to master and control. Sometimes managing a body feels overwhelming. Impulses and intense emotions threaten stability, inhibit progress and may even destroy life, mine or others. Yes, I felt I took on a huge responsibility when I chose to incarnate in a body, especially a human body. Humans feel emotions at an increased level of intensity, far beyond most other humanoid or "alien" forms.

I felt uncomfortable and completely disconnected from Source housed inside a form that had a "skin encapsulated self-sense." I felt a lot of bleed through, remembered far more of my past lives, concurrent and future lifetimes and existences on many levels than I should. Something seemed off.

I wondered, "Am I supposed to remember this much?" I recall someone told me before coming here that I need to prepare myself. Separation from universal consciousness feels rather complete here on Earth on this dimensional plane because the thick skin of the human form prevents penetration and unintentional transference of deep or intense emotional energies.

Our creators manipulated our DNA through genetic experimentation and hybridization to limit our intelligence, deny our longevity, suppress our immune system and program our ability to resist their commands. They blocked 256 genetic strands whose functions remain a mystery. Limitations and the drive to overcome limits drive our desires and maximize potential, increases diversification.

The human form evolved over time and as a result of many years of manipulation and programming. Humans changed over time by divine intervention (interventionism rather than evolution).

Each generation of geneticists fine-tuned and perfected their creations. They added, changed, mixed and remixed DNA in endless variations to create the desired effects of the creator. Mistakes were made. Corrections attempted. The end result of millions of years of interference and intervention by thousands of species, the human form represents the hope of the continuum. Human beings hold within their form the energies of the entire continuum. Within them resides the totality of all existence. Humans resonate and express within one form the divine concept of "heaven on earth", which symbolizes polarity concepts such as high/low, light/dark, separate/one, projection/acceptance, and war/peace.

I chose to come in to make changes to the timeline and the existing paradigm of death, separation and destruction. War, the enemy of all logical, rational, conscious beings seemed natural, almost second nature for these human beings.

This level of separation felt wrong and seemed illogical. Why did Earth and its human creatures feel so separate from each other that they demonized and projected, polluted and brutalized, hurt and harmed which threatened to extinct not only themselves, but all life? Illogical.

I must dive down in here personally and hit the restart button to set this out-of-balance planet and her beings on a correction course. I need to find the answers myself so as to not interfere in the process of
discovery. Unconscious, I suffer amnesia like all the

tourists who come here. No one gets to stay here forever.

For the first time I really connected with the babe. I stared out the eyes, allowed the iris to adjust to the light. I felt the air on my skin, adjusted to the temperature. I toyed with my arms and legs, played with balance to the point I would almost fall. But I caught myself for this time I needed to be inside and feel all I could as this human baby.

"Oh no, not here again!" I exclaimed out loud. Oh my, what a strange sound that came out of my throat. Was that really my voice? We really need to work on that.

3. Refusal of the Call: The hero tries to refuse the adventure because she's afraid.
Aug 1954 – when First I stood up, I said, *No, Not here again!*

I stayed this time, intent on integrating more and get acclimated to this new experience. Unattached to this form, I'd slip out and travel again whenever the baby slept. I went back to my Ninmah form I left in the Halls of Amenti. I love Ninmah. As Ninmah I've been through a lot. As Ninmah I love everyone which when Janet reviews her Ninmah self she admires that part of her which makes her such a cool soul and a good person. Those things she endured shaped her consciousness and transformed her into the awesome being she became.

With 256 strands of my DNA deactivated and my human brain so small, only that which allowed me to function as a human remained. Unable to retain much due to the human incarnation process, the core essence of my eternal-self remained to oversee the lifetime.

Ninmah encompasses the grand total of all her experiences and incarnations that came before, always remains Ninmah at her core no matter where she incarnates and the same applies to Janet. Yet for this "experiment" in consciousness, we agreed to amnesia and deactivated DNA, the parameters of the experience.

How can I reach my goal where I learn how to circumnavigate the brain wipe and reactivate the deactivated DNA from within form from within the primarily unconscious body? If I, Janet can achieve this, I can teach the others and eventually figure out how to reach the masses and wake up the world before the atomic clock ticks its last and kaboom, planet Earth meets a very sad and untimely end.

I had to play it safe, be careful, not reveal too much yet keep my wits about me and learn enough so I'm effective in my mission to save us all. What a huge task I've agreed to do.

But, I shall acquire allies along the way. Sometimes I feel lonely. However, thank Goddess, Source, my guides, ETs and angels always watch over me. On my journey through life I'll meet all these aspects of myself and also the apparent others I'll grow to love. The adventure begins. Ready or not, here I am.

I slept a lot. I came in and out, felt mostly bored. I do appreciate the people in my life and recognize they did their best to treat me nice and help me raise myself. My parents, always preoccupied, left me alone far too much for my own good. I felt lonely, abandoned. Loneliness has a purpose. It sparked my creativity and permitted time for extraterrestrials, angels and interdimensional beings to interact with me and helped develop vital skills for survival and growth.

I thought some foods tasted good. Others I couldn't stand. I felt quite annoyed that I needed diapers, one of the roughest parts of infancy. Now and again someone would stick me with a pin. Those who pricked me, intentionally or not probably felt resentful towards a squealing baby who couldn't contain her own body fluids. I decided to toilet train myself as soon as possible because at times resentment felt personal and intentional.

One final day when I woke up to poop-filled diapers, I felt so disgusted with myself I vowed I'd master control of my body functions immediately. No more did I defecate in my pants. In a very short time I mastered urinary control. My parents took full credit for having trained their daughter at such a young age.

I felt proud of myself that I accessed that part of me that knew how to do it from previous incarnations. The other parts of pre-existence may have been blocked. But at least I retained some of the important parts that definitely made my life much easier to handle.

Months later I practiced taking my body with my spirit and managed to levitate around my room. My mother had a second crib in the dining room on the wall closest to where the furnace vents ran behind it making it the warmest spot in the house. My mother protected me from the brutal, Pennsylvania winters with temperatures so cold the pipes burst in our home.

Braving the chill of the room outside warm blankets, I flew around the room once then returned to my crib with a plop and a giggle. I felt joyous, liberated from the constraints of my infant body which limited my ability to express myself authentically. My body imprisoned me, confined me to my skin. Unable to access the immortal being, the extraterrestrial in human form that exists within me, I felt sad and resentful.

Momentarily freed from my meat skin, I flew again. Once again I landed hard. Elated, I squealed and laughed even harder.

My mother intensely focused on laundry she washed in a wringer washer and hung on hangers she hoisted with a broom and hung on the open pipes that snaked across the kitchen ceiling, wondered what I found so amusing. She emerged from the kitchen just in time to catch me mid-flight during my third voyage around the room. She dropped the wet cloth in her hand and screamed. I can only imagine what she thought. I could smell her fear across the room.

From that moment forward she never saw me in the same light again. She feared me, her demon seed and spawn of Satan himself. Still, I felt deep down she loved me. But at the same time she hated me for I threatened her sanity and challenged her reality.

In response I stopped playing, ceased laughing and in fact I never levitated again so as to not upset her. Too late, our relationship forever tarnished, our interactions remained uncomfortable and strained throughout the years. I also spoke in language terms way beyond children my age. She could overlook one thing. But she realized add levitating to advanced language skills equates to a demon child, not a baby.

Forty plus years later at the Prophet's Conference in Santa Fe, NM a man approached the mic to ask a question of the speaker that just finished presenting on stage. But instead of asking a question the man told a story about how he levitated as a toddler. Raised by nuns in an orphanage, he described how he zoomed around the place and defiantly laughed as the nuns chased him with a broom yelles and attempted to catch him. The rebellion went on years until one day he had enough. His spirit broke. Beaten, brutalized and shamed, he suddenly stopped and from that day forward never flew again.

His testimonial deeply moved the audience. The man, visibly shaken from the intensity of his recall and difficulty sharing such intimate and potentially ill-received details of his life, he struggled to gather his composure. He cleared his throat then bravely asked the audience if anyone else remembered levitating; please meet him in the back of the room by the door on the far left.

I had repressed my levitation memories, shamed by the pain I caused my mother when she had such an intense, negative reaction to my flying. I turned to my husband, Sasha. Sasha saw in my eyes what I wanted and replied, "Of course." He knew the testimony awakened my memories and I had to go speak with that man.

I grabbed my sweater and hurriedly made my way to the rear past the crowd that began to fill the isles as they made their way to the exit during the break. When I reached the designated spot, a small crowd had gathered. I counted quickly under my breath before anyone had time to speak and we numbered 12 plus the man who spoke.

I felt shocked and amazed. I thought it impossible that so many people remembered levitating. What magic spell did our questioner break by speaking the unspeakable out loud? I wondered later, "Could levitation be a natural human ability stifled as a result of fear and shame generated by fearful adults? Adults, like my mother, relentlessly attack gifted children generation after generation. By an unspoken agreement, people not known to one another, maintained the box of ignorance which contains us all.

My mother frightened, insane, irrational, endangered me. Unbeknown to me the decision to stifle me came from unknown authorities in the continuum much wiser than me. My higher-self agreed to remain always connected to divine source and actively engaged with "the other side" and the realms and dimensions I traveled when asleep.

Far too dangerous to do otherwise the committee and I agreed to take the awareness and memories I have of my connection to everything and suppress them deeper within my subconscious. Unless the Janet personality dominated and was the controlling persona, Mother may slip from her weak hold on her own sanity and an unfortunate "accident" would befall young Janny Banny. While Father worked and Brother Bill and Sister Louise attended school all day, Mom had me in her mercy.

Before my mother's life ended, I managed to create a friendship with her. I loved my mother, but I came to realize early on that she was mentally ill and couldn't control herself. I learned to love unconditionally without expectations that my parents would act "normally". My father returned from WWII with a serious case of PTSD. My mother was mind-controlled and crazy with an operating person who could appear sane but somewhat eccentric to her community. Unbelievably my mother was very popular. She treated my brother and sister rather well. No one would believe how she treated me when we were alone so I learned to keep my thoughts to myself.

EXPERIENCERS CONSCIOUS CONTACTEES

THE GRIM REAPER
Janet Kira Lessin

1958 to 1966:
I fought GEORGE for my soul

I've long repressed the following story because it's so outlandish, even for me, that I've kept it to myself. Over time when I felt safe I shared it with a few, very special friends (like my husband). But now's it's time for me to come even further out of the closet. So here we are.

When I was a child I saw a being materialized in my neighbors' backyard. I would feel something was about to happen. The energy would shift, the air currents falter, like the temperature drop and air current change that you can feel just before a summer's thunderstorm. I stood frozen in awe and disbelief as the air itself shimmered like water parting and this creature vibrated through the portal and gradually became solid. At first he appeared wearing an 1840's undertakers' outfit with a stovepipe hat and tails, like a character out of a B movie about the Wild West.

Then the undertaker would morph and become an enormous, grotesque figure in a black monk's cloak, hood draped over his head barely revealing a face so hideous it took years for me to pull it into my conscious memory. Resembling Death, the Ghost from Scrooge's Christmas future, the creature radiated an energy that one could only describe as evil.

Terror gripped me completely I froze in my steps. Death's mind touched mine as he attempted to seize me and take me back with him to wherever he came from. I don't know how I knew that, only that he conveyed his intentions to be telepathically. He let me knew he meant me harm. Telepathically we battled. I fought with all I had and what I knew was the salvation of my very soul. I as a seven year old battled my version of Goliath. What chance did I have against a seven foot monster from another world?

I don't know how I broke free, but somehow when he thought "Oh that's who you are," his spell on me was broken. I was released, paralysis gone and fled with all the swiftness my adrenalin-driven feet could muster. Up the back steps, I threw open the door, slammed it shut and collapsed my back upon it, my heart raced as I grasped for air. It's amazing I didn't faint, but perhaps I did. Who knows? Mother-Nature mercifully released her kindly chemicals to make me forget. Otherwise I think I would have lost my sanity trying to cope.

Next week, next month, next year, who knows, once again I'd saunter down the alley and my Friend" would appear and to do battle again. "Oh no, you again!" I screamed in my head, amazed that I'd fallen again into this trap. I'd get free, I'd run, I'd collapse, I'd forget, over and over, year after year like some sick mixture of "Groundhog Day" and "Beetlejuice" The final episode occurred the summer when I was twelve. That final time for some reason, I did not forget. But I wished I could somehow.

Years later my sister, brother and I shared "ghost stories" of the house we were raised in. We went into the house to clean up after paramedics. That morning medics had rushed our parents to nearby hospitals where Mom and Dad hovered near death. Shell shocked from the trauma, exhausted, we collapsed on the floor.

We shared our pain at the possibility of losing both our parents. After shedding many tears, we stopped and looked around us, and realized we hadn't been together in the house where we were raised, alone without the folks in over twenty years. Nostalgia took over and we began to share our deepest feelings of what it was like to be raised in that house by those parents.

During the course of the conversation we each began to reveal the terror we'd so long kept to ourselves. Each of us had experienced episodes with "ghosts." Some funny, some violent, we confessed our worst nightmares that we'd hoped were mere hallucinations.

Amazed at the horrors each of us survived at the hands of discarnates, we were relieved to finally be able to tell the truth. 800 Orchard was very, very haunted. A portal, a vortex allowed beings and beasties from near and beyond to saunter though our house, our bedrooms and even, sometime through us.

THE UNDERTAKER

Much to my amazement my older sister Louise met "George" (as I had dubbed him). "Death" and "grim reaper" no longer seemed to fit after I defeated him so often. I gave him a comical name and it stuck.

In the late 60s my sister and her boyfriend parked the car in the back alley to make out. Louise saw George first as he moved towards them wearing his undertakers outfit. She alerted John who screamed upon seeing him, "We've got to get the hell out of here," at the top of his lungs.

I listened slack-jawed as Louise recounted how John, terrified, dropped his keys trying to get them in the ignition. Terrified, he yelled, Louise screamed. I envisioned a scene like something out of a teenage horror flick as Louise described how John finally located the keys he had fumbled onto the floor while George crept ever and ever closer. Miraculously John got the key in the ignition. The car hesitated. Then finally it started just in the nick of time as George reached for the car's handle.

I had hoped I had imagined George. At this point in time I still dismissed it all as I figured these hallucinations must be genetic. Surely, my family is crazy. But then life, synchronistic as it is, was soon to bring other alien incidents to my attention which we'll get to later in this book.

Pg. 9 Blue Blood, True Blood, Stewart explains how it all began; "In the beginning, God existed as mind and nothing else. All there was, is, and ever will be, is mind. It has no idea where it came from. It only knows that it always existed and has no end. It allows for all thought and ideas to come to fruition somewhere within itself. It allows any and all events to occur, so in this way it knows itself. It does not directly interfere with its thought-creations. It does not have an agenda. It does not judge, interfere, or change anything that is already created. It allows for freewill of all creations within itself.

In this way, all possibilities unfold. Nothing is ever stopped from being. Humans may judge events and other things as good or bad, positive or negative, but to the God-Mind, they are all simply pieces of itself."

Here-in lies the keys we need to free us from the Godspell. But like the characters in the Matrix who had to decide whether they wanted to choose the red or the blue pill, chose truth or stay in their old beliefs that were familiar and comforting, you may want to take a deep look before expanding outside of your box. For once you grow; you're not going to fit back in it again.

Stewart's not alone in the theory that there are many species populating the universe. Many psychic channels seem to converge on the same information even though they attempt to discredit one another. When we look at the evidence: physical remnants unearthed from ancient ruins, huge structures, anomalies and monoliths located around the world and writings carved in stone, apparently Earth has been visited by most of the major races. Ironically,

The story behind the creation of this solar system supports the theory of a major war which caused massive death and destruction. When war moved to Solaris' solar system, the battle that ensued ripped away Mars' atmosphere and destroyed a planet called Maldek, which became the asteroid belt.

Sitchin and Swerdlow both describe elaborate battles involving the planets. Sitchin describes a celestial battle, where worlds collide create great change and havoc through conflicting orbits and gravitational pull. Swerdlow involves Humanoids and Reptilians slinging planets in his descriptions of the cosmic wars. There are obvious discrepancies.

Sitchin does not mention the Dracos or other races on Earth before the Anunnaki arrived 450,000 years ago. Sitchin does not really take into account places such as Lemuria, Mu and Atlantis. There are a number of possible explanations for this. Perhaps the Anunnaki were unaware of the existence of other races and the story they report of the planetary battle emerges from their mythology.

They obviously knew something of the history of the cosmos, for they knew there was gold in the asteroid belt and on Earth. Perhaps Sitchin knows more than he's telling us. He may be deliberately holding back the whole story in order to sell more books, or perhaps the government is only letting him reveal bits and pieces at a time and only the bits they want revealed. Icke seems to think Sitchin is part of the Illuminati.

However, for my theory, I'd like to explore the hypothesis that the Anunnaki were initially unaware of other species of advanced life inhabiting Earth.

Yahweh and the secret societies that followed (like the Knights Templar and the Illuminati) fostered dogmatic religions and encouraged psychological warfare using religions to polarize people and further divide humanity. Wars ensued through the ages, brother against brother, and nation against nation.

Today we find ourselves fighting over fictitious borders while simultaneously separated from our feminine by our pathetic patriarchal religions. Raised by women that we instinctually know are just as smart as our fathers and therefore equal, and taught to suppress our own feminine selves which we feel, it's no wonder we're a world acting out our neurosis in violence and war. It's time to stop the craziness. Time to become conscious.

So what we've created in our consensus reality is Trump and Hitler. What's the reason behind such a manifestation and is such negative disregard for consciousness necessary for our pleasure?

In "War is What Gives Us Meaning, "author such and such states that war creates commonality between those who would otherwise never know each other nor give a damn if they do or not. Is the major reason war is so juicy, so attractive, because it gives life meaning and allows the participants to experience unity consciousness?

If that's so, then can we simply create other models to achieve that experience of unity consciousness, models that are as life-affirming as facing death, as exciting as killing others in combat, as intense as dominating and controlling another to do our will or die?

GEORGE THE REPTILIAN

Years later and finally after great resistance from a part of me that just didn't want to know, I finally decided to read "Children of the Matrix," by David Icke. Several people recommended his books to me and typical me, I resisted. Then one day at Borders I happened upon the book. The cover was so intriguing, it caught my eye. And once I started reading it, I couldn't put it down. Despite its massive size, 457 pages, I consumed it in a couple days. Now that's an indicator of a good book. David Icke and his books have totally transformed my reality and helped me make sense of a life full of riddles, mysteries and confusion.

I owe David a huge debt of gratitude and my husband and I were blessed to meet him years ago and hang out a while with him here at our home in Maui, Hawaii. David's research has rocked my world and the world of many others due to his exposition of the reptilian presence on Earth. Because of this groundbreaking work, I feel brave enough to discuss a topic that was once taboo to most of humanity. Revealing the Draconian extraterrestrial influence and interference in humanity's evolution, history and politics is critical to discovering who and what humanity is at our core and what's actually happening here on Earth.

I'll never forget how I felt when I finally recovered a hidden thread of my psyche, an image repressed for so long to protect my fragile self. When I looked at the image on the bottom of page 192 (which is a picture of a Reptilian with the caption "Artist Clive Burrows produced this impression of a shape-shifted Ted Heath conducting a ritual at Burnham Beeches from descriptions provided by the woman who witnessed this scene in the early 1970s)," a veil lifted in my mind.

Suddenly I was thrust back in time. I found myself back in the alley facing my neighbor's back yard and suddenly George emerged from the portal. Once again he attempted to suck out my soul. As I looked at the drawing on the page before me, my eyes were drawn to the eyes in the drawing. As I zoomed in the eyes in the drawing faded and George's eyes replaced them and George himself was looking at me! I gasped, shocked as the eyes in the picture merged, and became one and the same.

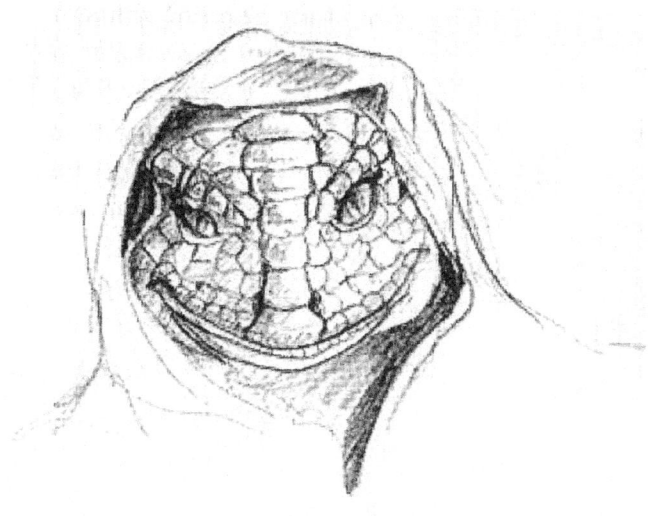

Transported back through time, my heart raced as I realized those eyes in my minds 'eye were alive, three dimensional and in full, living color. They pierced through me, set my panicking heart racing. My entire body on fire, adrenaline firing signals to my extremities, my mind screamed, "Run or be killed. Run or you'll die."

I flashed back to the now. When I initially read the book I glanced past the image on page 182. I needed the cloak on the image from page 192 to reconnect to the image repressed in my mind. The caption reads, "The three main varieties of extraterrestrials, reported in abductions and other experiences. This is one of the many types of reptilian beings and this image was painted from ancient and modern descriptions by artist Hilary Reed." I stared at that image. And there he was, at last, George fully restored in my mind. At last I remembered the entire episode. Amazed and somewhat relieved, finally I remembered. It was a long haul for I had blocked his face for over 40 years.

Years later guidance told me to go get a copy of the Harry Potter DVDs and take a look. I resisted because it was a children's story, and I really am so busy, how could I justify watching such a thing. But I've learned to trust my guidance and the episode I picked was the exact one I needed to see. I forget the name of the movie, but in this one poor Harry fought the grim reapers as they tried to suck his soul from his being. Harry couldn't take it and collapsed in a heap.

After watching it to the end, I reflected on that scene. It was far too close to what actually happened to me. I wondered if J.K. Rowling was someone on the inside track of some secret society information and she was getting it out to the world in her stories. Or maybe she wasn't conscious and was fed information like many others.

But silly as it was, I felt somewhat proud of myself that I managed to break free from the reaper rather than faint like our hero Harry of Potter fame.

Little Janny Banny escaped, soul intact retaining her wits. I had encountered the beast, time and again and despite his efforts, he could never win, steal my soul, stop my heart, and take my final breath.

A sense of relief came over me. Somehow I was no longer afraid. Granted part of me judged my fear as senseless, that things like that couldn't really exist. But from this perspective looking at reality from this piece of the elephant, if George and his kind indeed do exist, I know consciousness runs through all beings. While George may have intended me ill (it seems logical that he did), there is kindness in the image on page 182 of the "Children of the Matrix" and malice on the face of the one in the ritual on page 192. Perhaps like humans, reptilians are as diverse as us. Maybe they too have their Hitler and Christ.

For some reason I felt peace and believed in the goodness of all beings. I seek that in others and am committed to create that reality of love for all.

ADDENDUM

Memories are like the layers of an onion. Only this onion sometimes took years to peel. When I was preparing a PowerPoint for a conference, I addressed the issue of George once again. He's a very interesting character and for some reason he's very important in my life. While searching for images and creating the presentation suddenly I remembered, George meant me no harm.

I was used to telepathic communication with the grey aliens and other species that touched the mind almost like an embrace, a soft kiss or even a tickle. But reptilians are so powerful and less sensitive because of their nature. When George attempted to communicate with me mind to mind, his energy was over the top, intense, harsh and somewhat brutish. At that time I was a very young and somewhat fragile and sickly child. When George touched my mind with his, it felt so intense, I thought he was trying to kill me, rip my soul from my body and carry me off to Hell (a Christian concept I had been taught at that time).

But upon reviewing what actually happened, I realize that George was simply an ambassador of sorts and I overreacted to his appearance. I am a representative of the Earth and humanity (since I'm now incarnated in human form) and when I'm in my external self and awareness of my role in existence, I am a much more powerful, wise and knowledgeable being. I travel the universe, work on other worlds and contribute far more than this human self can consciously remember. I come back from my astral travels at night where I work my "other job" and live my "other life", and I'm left with an awareness of my role in the continuum. But my Janet body, ego and self-sense is not nearly ready to handle such energy. I go to these other realms, dimensions and worlds all the time. I'm so busy at night; I divide myself and cover a lot of territory.

When I awaken I'm in bliss, fully recharged and ready to handle the complexities and difficulties of my human life. And there's also much comfort, beauty, love and joy as Janet. Yet I am also Joy, Ninmah, Kira and much more.

George was either unaware of my sensitive child Janet self or he was aware and incapable of sufficiently adjusting his energy to match mine. Looking back I realize he was making adjustments each time he encountered me over the years.

But I was so fully immersed in my Janet self, by the time I integrated all my encounters with George, the damage was done. So another strategy for communicating with me was developed over time. Subconscious communication never ceased. Conscious communications designed to help me integrate all my levels of existence, my many incarnations that exist in many times and on many planets and my multi-dimensional selves continue to this day. That's why I can communicate with you, finally come totally out of the proverbial closet and disclose to you what's really going on. As always, you are to evaluate, judge, discern and incorporate into yourself and your own awareness that which serves you and your loved ones to the highest good. Don't ever let anyone else define your own reality. That's actually the purpose of incarnating in worlds, to co-create with God Source and diversify existence.
Somewhere there's a reality that's win-for-all where no one is left behind and everyone gets their needs met

while there's plenty to do to make the process of incarnating in form interesting enough to keep doing.

I see the monsters of my childhood morph into intelligent beings of higher consciousness

George, I realize that I was wrong and I beg your forgiveness. You are actually a dear beloved, a soul that's worthy of much kindness and consideration. I, a young and foolish, unconscious human child reacted horribly and judged you unfairly. George, you're beautiful. This picture is a representation of how I perceived you before and how I see you now.

George, you're most definitely a hunk! I clearly see now that you radiate love from your heart that is open, kind, loving and gentle. One final thing I realize is that George is a regular at the council meetings I attend on a regular basis.

Over time memories return and information permitted to come forth to the surface and be released from my subconscious to the world. The same is happening with many experiencers. We are indeed blessed as we face incredible, somewhat magical times as we countdown to disclosure, the truth which comes from experiencers everywhere. These ambassadors that have been selected by extraterrestrials bring forth into the light the golden age of Aquarius, promised to humanity so long ago.

JANET KIRA LESSIN

DANCE OF THE SOULS: PIERCE THE VEIL

We constantly change roles and partners like an old-fashioned country square dance. We go round and round, lifetime after lifetime. We are parent/child, husband/wife, brother/sister, mother/father, friend/foe, lover/enemy, hero/villain, boss/employee, master/slave, perpetrator/victim, maimer/maimed, killer/killed over and over throughout eternity. Life's not limited to life here on Earth, human forms, planets, dimensions, solar systems, galaxies or vibratory frequencies. We can be anywhere. In many ways we are everywhere all at once.

"In the Dance of the Souls: Pierce the Veil," author Janet Kira Lessin explores one soul's existence, her own, as she travels through eternity and interacts with her twin flame and souls mates, those with whom she has shared and interacted with since the beginning, shaping and forming all elements of reality. Together they create it all. The play is performed and they are it all – stage, script writer, producer, director, actor, lights, camera, action. Their dance creates experiences, diversity, emotions and all that encompasses life and existence itself. In the course of co-creation souls eventually become conscious and realize their oneness, that they are eternally connected and the I that is me that is we is the I that I am that is all that I am.

The story's auto-biographical, not limited to one life, inclusive of all spanning billions of years to the dawn of the creation of the Earth herself. I, the author tell it all, bare my soul for if the tale is not told now, then when? How can I possibly have ever lived if I am not somewhere in time truthful with what life has been? Just because what I have experienced is outside the traditional box, does not invalidate it or make it less than other existences which were more 'normal' and conformed to traditional expectations of what life should be.

ISBN 9781480143173

FREE Experiencer Research Study

The Dr. Edgar Mitchell Foundation for Research into Extraterrestrial Encounters, or FREE, was formally incorporated as a Not for Profit Research Organization on July 15, 2015. FREE was co-founded by the late Apollo Astronaut, Dr. Edgar Mitchell, and Harvard Professor of Astrophysics, Dr. Rudy Schild.

FREE has been established by various retired Ph.D. Physicists, Ph.D. Scientists, Ph.D. Psychologists, Ph.D. Neuroscientists and lay researchers to facilitate investigations into **"UFO related contact experiences with non-human intelligent beings and its associated paranormal activity, from a grounded and rigorous scientific foundation"**.

FREE is undertaking the first ever long term comprehensive ACADEMIC research study on the UFO related Contact Phenomena-- The FREE Experiencer Research Study. The Co-Chairs of this research study, Dr. Jon Klimo, a retired professor of Transpersonal Psychology and one of the world's leading academics on the "Paranormal". The other Co-Chair is Dr. Bob Davis, a retired professor of Neuroscience and Consciousness. Our primarily focus will be on scientific investigation, through surveys and interviews of individuals who have had UFO related contact experiences with non-human intelligent beings, and to compare this group with individuals that have had other types of "paranormal contact experiences" through the following: NDEs, OBEs, Hallucinogenic/Entheogenic natural substances, hypnotic regression, Mystical Meditation Travel, Channeling, Remote Viewing, and other human encounters with non-human intelligence and related paranormal contact experiences.

Our research study involves two comprehensive quantitative surveys, Phase 1 and Phase 2, totally more than 600 questions and 2 qualitative research instruments, Phase 3 and 4. Phase 3 is a qualitative instrument and involves written responses to 70 open ended questions. Phase 4 involves a formal structured interview that will be orally recorded and transcribed. All 4 phases will be completely anonymous.

ANONYMITY: Confidentiality and Anonymity is extremely important to us. As a participant for our 3 surveys and formal interview, the Participant has a choice to remain completely "**ANONYMOUS**". There will not be a way for anyone to find out who is the Participant, where they live, or any other personal information to identify you. In addition, the Interviewer will not have any personal identifying information about you. Instead, the Participant will be given a Respondent Number. During your Interview you will not be asked any information to identify who you are (name, address, or other sensitive personal ID information). All of the interviews will be audio recorded and later transcribed to paper via appropriate software. This is the reason why it is important to maintain complete anonymity. After the voice files have been transcribed, they will be destroyed. What will be left is a transcribed document that will not have any personal identifying information except for the Respondent Number.

LINK TO PHASE 1 SURVEY:
https://www.surveymonkey.com/s/LZW6VZP

Should you have any question about our research study please send us an email **INFO@EXPERIENCER.ORG**

Dr. Rudy Schild, Executive Director of FREE

The Foundation for Research into Extraterrestrial Encounters

Email: INFO@EXPERIENCER.ORG
Website: EXPERIENCER.ORG

EPILOGUE

According to the latest surveys millions have been abducted by aliens. One contactee revealed that he was told by ET that all human beings are taken at punctuated periods of their lives, tested and analyzed for various factors known only by ET, and then some are chosen for ongoing contact throughout their lives. Based on that information we're all experiencers yet don't know it because the memories of our encounters are blocked.

Abductees are among the groups that are studied by Experiencer organizations such as F.R.E.E. aka The Edgar Mitchell Foundation for Research into Extraterrestrial Encounters. According to their website (www.experiencer.org), experiencer categories include: NDEs (near death experiences), OBEs (out of body experiences), Hallucinogenic/Entheogenic natural substances, hypnotic regression, Mystical Meditation Travel, Channeling, Remote Viewing, and human encounters with non-human intelligence, and related paranormal contact experiences. Thus, the focus is not solely on UFO contact experiences but on all types of paranormal contact experiences.

"*Experiencers Conscious Contactees, Volume I*" is the first of an ongoing collection of experiencer stories which features stories of experiencers who remember contact. In this book we focus on all of the above plus ET treaties, experiencer hypnotherapy, alien contact, paranormal activity, UFOs, Moon and Mars anomalies, MILABS (military abductions), secret space programs, breakaway civilizations, missing time, levitation, extraordinary abilities, prophetic visions, telepathy (telepathic communication), NDE's, astral projection, reptilians, greys, ancient aliens, Anunnaki, blue beings, angels and other non-human entities and spiritual guides.

Join us as we open your mind, expand consciousness, awaken humanity and guide us all, human and not to the Golden Age of Aquarius, the age of enlightenment promised long ago and with your assistance as co-creators with God Source, delivered to us just in the nick of time.

We need your stories which encompass the totality of humanity, the human story that spans the ages and includes all generations, our ancestors and how we came to be. With your assistance we create disclosure for all humans and with disclosure we free ourselves from the negative, perverted matrix.

Disclosure means technologies that give us clean, free energy, cures for diseases, longevity if not physical immortality, avenues to clean up the entire planet, an invitation for humanity to join the Federation of Planets and much more. These things may not be immediately forthcoming for there are forces against us that do not want humanity to succeed. But, humanity has as many if not more allies then enemies. We join forces with beings of love and light and focus on our goal--to free humanity from the perverted matrix, the negative timeline, the slave planet quarantined for the protection of all beings (however you symbol it). Remember who we are in the grand scheme of things and join our galactic family of souls that came into existence to co-create experiences, bodies and planets in which our souls could play, learn, grow, evolve and become all that we imagined we could be. We plant the seeds for this path which is essential for the survival of not only humanity but all life on Earth. We initially set the course for planetary destruction with our stupidity and carelessness. We now get to play the hero to our own villain and rescue the world.

Contact us at aquarianradio@gmail.com. Give us feedback and your ideas. We need help. This cannot possibly be done alone. Come on our radio talk shows. You can use your real name or not. Tell your stories. Write them up. If you need help writing up your story we can interview you, get it transcribed, and assist you in the process to get your story out to the world in as many media formats as possible.

Proceeds go towards putting on regional conferences around the globe, staring in the United States and expanding to all continents. When we gather together, share breath, look deep into each other's eyes all the way to our souls, we alter the morphogenic field and create a more kind and loving grid. We shift timelines to a positive one. We change reality to one that supports higher consciousness and awareness, respects life.

Join us as we begin our journey to the stars. We need all of us to get there.

ABOUT THE EDITOR
Janet Kira Lessin

Janet is an author (http://www.amazon.com/author/janetkiralessin), educator, experiencer, contactee, researcher, conference presenter, conference organizer, radio show host, workshop leader and counselor. She and her husband, Dr. Sasha Lessin, facilitate experiencers at conferences, in skype groups and in their growth center in Maui, Hawaii. She works with those who channel, who engage in shamanic journeywork, or who use tantric ritual to access the superconscious.

Likewise, her specialties include tarrying with those who experience abduction, astral contact or paranormal activity, who belong to alien contact groups, or who have supernormal and nature guides. Janet's practice encompasses those who access the dead, experienced near death experiences, who get powerful psychic intimations, who experience themselves and others as multidimensional. In her practice, Janet helps ground those in contact with the metacosmic void.

Janet presents PowerPoints based on her life as an Experiencer (which began at birth), plus information based on her research which includes presentations based on the Anunnaki, ancient aliens, Ufology, Experiencers and her work as a counselor with Dr. Sasha Lessin dealing with clients who've experienced paranormal and ET contact plus non-ordinary states of consciousness (such as astral travel, remote viewing, shamanic journeys, etc.).

Janet presents solo or with her beloved husband, Dr. Sasha Lessin. Janet and Sasha love to present together. Together they facilitate workshops, experiencer groups and private counseling sessions. Sessions, workshops and educational tutorials are based on the Anunnaki, ancient aliens, tantra, spiritual emergence, relationship counseling, life coaching, personal growth counseling, kundalini awakening and more.

At 13, saddened with the hypocrisy of religion, Janet embarked on a spiritual path–read hundreds of books on the paranormal, psychology and consciousness expansion and, in seminars and counseling, overcame her childhood abuse issues and learned to help others.

In 1997, Janet wed Dr. Sasha Lessin and began teaching with him. In their work with experiencers, contactees and psychics, the Lessins adapt methods from Holotropic Breathwork, Existential Analysis, Tantra, Voice Dialogue, Gestalt, Hypnotherapy, Past and Future Life Regression and Progression as well as Imago Work. They teach experiencers how to center themselves and integrate the energies they access in extraterrestrial and inter-dimensional, as well as paranormal experiences.

Janet is the author of "Dance of the Souls: Pierce the Veil" Janet is the co-author of "Anunnaki: Legacy of the Gods & Anunnaki: False Gods." She's the editor of the Experiencers anthology series of books.

The Lessins teach and employ hypnosis, Jungian Past life Therapy, Holotropic Breathworker, Yoga, Tantra, Spirit Releasement, Extraterrestrial and exopolitical deprogramming, Voice Dialogue Centering, Existential Analysis, Gestalt Therapy, Spiritual growth and Psychosynthesis.

Websites:
www.schoolofcounseling.org
www.extraterrestrialcontact.com
www.enkispeaks.com
www.schooloftantra.com
www.worldpolyamoryassociation.com
www.worldpeaceassociation.com
www.ninmah.com
www.experiencersnetwork.com
www.aliencontactorganization.com
www.aquarianradio.com

We also have many related pages and groups on Facebook and other social networks on counseling, spirituality, tantra, relationship choice, extraterrestrial and paranormal contact. The Lessins specialize in clearing intensives, facilitated regression, progression and shamanic journeywork.

The Lessins are available for in-person, phone or skype sessions.

Janet Kira and Dr. Sasha Lessin
1371 Malaihi Road, Wailuku, HI 96793
808-244-4103

Email:
sashalessinphd@aol.com
janetlessin@gmail.com
808-244-4103

EXPERIENCERS CONSCIOUS CONTACTEES

In "*Experiencers Conscious Contactees*, Volume I" we relate our adventures with extraterrestrials. We start with U.S. President Eisenhower's treaty with ETs, Dr. Lessin's method of hypnotic exploration of extraterrestrial and paranormal contact. Then our authors recount their alien and paranormal contacts, UFO briefings, and recovery of uncensored UFOs, Moon and Mars anomalies. We relate our military (MILAB) abductions and revelations of the secret space programs, breakaway civilizations, and time travel. We share what happened in missing time and describe our encounters with levitation, extraordinary abilities, astral projection, prophetic visions and telepathy. Experiencers also relate our encounters with nonhuman entities, Anunnaki, blue beings, spiritual guides and angels. We discuss our contacts with Reptilians, Greys, Agarthans and our own hidden subpersonalities. Join us as we open your mind, expand consciousness, awaken humanity and guide us all, human and not to the Golden Age of Aquarius, the age of enlightenment promised long ago.

Edited By

Janet Kira Lessin

Featuring:

Korey Lavoie, Melinda Leslie, Miesha Johnston, Sherry Wilde, John M. Polk, Joan Hangarter, Hildegard Gmeiner, Barbara Jean Lindsey, Karen Christine Patrick, Bret Colin Sheppard, Rebecca Hardcastle Wright, Russell Scott Brinegar & Sasha Alex Lessin, Ph.D.

Made in the USA
Coppell, TX
30 June 2025